Books
are keys to wisdom's
treasure;
Books are paths
that upward lead;
Books are gates
to lands of pleasure
Books are friends,
Come, let us read
❖   ❖   ❖

CHRISTIAN BROTHERS

FRANCIS X. WEISER

The Christmas Book

ILLUSTRATED BY ROBERT FRANKENBERG

HARCOURT, BRACE AND COMPANY

NEW YORK

Library of Congress Catalog Card Number: 52-11344

IMPRIMI POTEST: William E. Fitzgerald, S.J., Provincial
NIHIL OBSTAT: Hugh F. Blunt, LL.D., Censor librorum
IMPRIMATUR: ✠ Richard J. Cushing, D.D., Archbishop of Boston

ACKNOWLEDGMENTS: To Edasi Publishers, Caracas, Venezuela, for permission to translate a carol, and to Pantheon Books for permission to use some of the music for carols from *The Trapp Family Book of Christmas Songs*. To Edward C. Currie for his assistance in research on carols and to the Rev. William A. Donaghy, S.J., the Rev. Gerard Barry, to Allan J. Doherty, and to Mary R. Geiger for help in preparing the manuscript.

The carols were translated by the author.

The notes referred to by number throughout the text are to be found at the end of the book.

Figures in parentheses after the names of persons indicate the year of death.

TO THE MEMORY OF A CHERISHED FRIEND
GEORG VON TRAPP
1880 - 1947

Foreword

Over the known world, about two thousand years ago, the victorious Roman eagle jealously brooded; Rome's irresistible armies had won the earth, her navies swept and scoured the seas, her coffers were swollen with tribute; but her fine, primitive virility was rotting into that decadence which Tacitus would so tersely sum up. Poets like Keats and minor disciples of Rousseau might look back longingly on those days which distance has haloed in enchantment; but the glory that was Greece and the splendor that was Rome had become bright garments, brocaded bandages over deep and fatal sores. The great masses of people were economically poor or enslaved, cruelty was a policy, and the mighty were blessed because they possessed the land. The world, in Augustine's summary, was moving slowly and inexorably toward the edge of perdition, and fear was the climate of man's normal living.

All this was changed because one night in a cattle shed, in a small town of a despised area dependent on the Imperial Province of Syria, a young girl gave birth to a boy Child. All history revolves around that event which is central in liturgy as it is in life. Christmas is the birthday of an era, the inauguration of a culture,

7

the beginning of a creed, the fountainhead of man's hope. ✗

I have herein tried to recall the origins and historical significance of these customs and ceremonies with which Christian men surrounded the birthday of their King, with the hope that it will warm the heart and bring closer to all who read it the real significance and meaning of our Christmas customs.

FRANCIS X. WEISER, S.J.

Weston College
Weston, Massachusetts

The First Christmas

The Birth of Jesus (Luke 2, 1-7) · Now it came to pass in those days, that there went forth a decree from Caesar Augustus that a census of the whole world should be taken. This first census took place while Cyrinus was governor of Syria. And all were going, each to his own town, to register.

And Joseph also went from Galilee out of the town of Nazareth into Judea to the town of David, which is called Bethlehem—because he was of the house and family of David—to register, together with Mary his espoused wife, who was with child. And it came to pass while they were there, that the days for her to be delivered were fulfilled. And she brought forth her firstborn son, and wrapped him in swaddling clothes, and laid him in a manger, because there was no room for them in the inn.

The Shepherds at the Crib (Luke 2, 8-20) · And there were shepherds in the same district living in the fields and keeping watch over their flock by night. And behold, an angel of the Lord stood by them and the glory of God shone round about them, and they feared exceedingly.

And the angel said to them, "Do not be afraid, for

behold, I bring you good news of great joy which shall be to all the people; for there has been born to you today in the town of David a Saviour, who is Christ the Lord. And this shall be a sign to you: you will find an infant wrapped in swaddling clothes and lying in a manger." And suddenly there was with the angel a multitude of the heavenly host praising God and saying,

"Glory to God in the highest,
and peace on earth among men
of good will."

And it came to pass, when the angels had departed from them into heaven, that the shepherds were saying to one another, "Let us go over to Bethlehem and see this thing that has come to pass, which the Lord has made known to us."

So they went with haste, and they found Mary and Joseph, and the babe lying in the manger. And when they had seen, they understood what had been told them concerning this child. And all who heard marveled at the things told them by the shepherds. But Mary kept in mind all these words, pondering them in her heart. And the shepherds returned, glorifying and praising God for all they had heard and seen, even as it was spoken to them.

The Magi (Matthew 2, 1-12) · Now when Jesus was born in Bethlehem of Judea, in the days of King Herod, behold, there came Magi from the East to Jerusalem, saying, "Where is the newly born king of the Jews? For we have seen his star in the East and have come to worship him." But when King Herod heard this, he was troubled, and so was all Jerusalem with him. And gathering together all the chief priests and Scribes of the people, he inquired of them where the Christ was to be born. And they said to him, "In Bethlehem of Judea; for thus it is written through the prophet,

'And thou, Bethlehem, of the land of Juda,
  art by no means least among the princes of Juda;
For from thee shall come forth a leader
  who shall rule my people of Israel.' "

Then Herod summoned the Magi secretly, and carefully ascertained from them the time when the star had appeared to them. And sending them to Bethlehem, he said, "Go and make careful inquiry concerning the child, and when you have found him, bring me word, that I too may go and worship him."

Now they, having heard the king, went their way. And behold, the star that they had seen in the East went before them, until it came and stood over the place where the child was. And when they saw the star they rejoiced exceedingly. And entering the house, they found the child with Mary his mother, and falling down they worshiped him. And opening their treasures they offered him gifts of gold, frankincense and myrrh. And

11

being warned in a dream not to return to Herod, they went back to their own country by another way.

The Innocents (Matthew 2, 16-18) · Then Herod, seeing that he had been tricked by the Magi, was exceedingly angry; and he sent and slew all the boys in Bethlehem and all its neighborhood who were two years and under, according to the time that he had carefully ascertained from the Magi. Then was fulfilled what was spoken through Jeremias the prophet, saying:

> "A voice was heard in Rama,
>   weeping and loud lamentation;
> Rachel weeping for her children,
>   and she would not be comforted,
>   because they are no more."

Contents

FOREWORD 7

INTRODUCTION The First Christmas 9

1. Gospel and History 17
2. Origin of the Feast 31
3. Christmas in the Middle Ages 36
4. Decline and Revival 43
5. The Midnight Mass 51
6. Ancient Hymns and Carols 55
7. Carols for Every Mood 60
8. Familiar Hymns and Carols 79
9. Nativity Plays 94
10. The Christmas Crib 105
11. Symbolic Lights and Fires 111
12. The Christmas Tree 117
13. Christmas Plants and Flowers 123
14. Breads and Pastries 135
15. The Christmas Dinner 142
16. The Battle of the Mince Pie 147
17. Saint Nicholas 152
18. The Significance of Exchanging Presents 157
19. Santa Claus 163
20. Cherished Customs—Old and New 167

REFERENCE NOTES 175

INDEX 179

The Christmas Book

CHAPTER 1

Gospel and History

The Year of Christ's Birth · Have you ever observed that the Gospel reports do not mention the year in which Christ was born? Even the few historical facts given by St. Luke and St. Matthew do not help to establish the year. The Evangelists recorded the actions and teachings of Christ as a catechetical sketch with no thought of days and dates to satisfy the later demands of scholars. The Apostles, of course, did not write as scientists and historians but as religious instructors.

When scholars finally approached the problem, there was so little to go on that an error was made. This happened in the sixth century when a learned monk in

Rome, Dionysius "the little" *Exiguus* (about 540), conceived the idea of introducing a Christian calendar. Reckoning historical events as best he could, he assigned the year one—the date of the birth of Jesus—to the year 754 after the founding of Rome. Actually he made a mistake of at least four years. It is now generally agreed by historians that King Herod "the Great" died within a few days of April first, in the year 4 B.C. It is known from the Gospel that at Herod's death Jesus was with Mary and Joseph in Egypt. From all available facts His age was then between six months and three years, so He must have been born between the years 7 B.C. and 4 B.C.

The modern world still follows and perpetuates the error of Dionysius Exiguus because it would be impossible at this late date to change and rearrange every event of history, every recorded time-table, all the dates in books and documents, for the last fourteen centuries. But to those who celebrate the central fact of Christ's birth it makes little difference whether the actual year of the Nativity was 6 or 5 B.C.

The Place of the Nativity · The Gospel tells us that Mary laid her child in a manger. Where was this manger? In the limestone area around Bethlehem are a number of natural caves which were used as shelters for animals. The fact that Christ was born in one of

18

these caves has been substantiated. As early as 160, St. Justin the Martyr, who himself was a native of Palestine, gave the clear testimony: "Joseph lodged in a certain cave near the village; and then, while they were yet there, Mary gave birth to the Christ and placed Him in a manger. . . ." [1]

The pagan Romans unwittingly helped to preserve the knowledge of the cave in which Christ was born, since from the time of Emperor Hadrian (138) to that of Constantine the Great (337) they deliberately desecrated the most sacred shrines of Christianity by establishing centers of pagan worship in these spots. They turned the place of Christ's birth into a grotto and grove of the god Adonis, a beautiful youth who, according to pagan legend, had been in love with the goddess Aphrodite (Venus) and was killed by a wild boar in the prime of his life. His death was mourned by worshipers in a ritual of wailing and mourning.

St. Jerome (420), who lived for a long time in Bethlehem, wrote about this desecration: "In the cave which had heard the tender wailings of the infant Christ, the lover of Venus was bemoaned." [2] The Christian writer Origen (about 250) stated at the beginning of the third century that even the pagans knew the grotto in which the Saviour was born and would point it out to the pilgrims. [3]

After his conversion to Christianity Emperor Constantine in 325 ordered that a magnificent church be

19

built over the cave. This basilica was almost ruined in the Samaritan revolt (521-528) and was restored by Emperor Justinian (565). The Persians, invading Palestine in 614, completely destroyed the Christian shrines at Nazareth and Jerusalem but respected the church of the Nativity in Bethlehem. According to an ancient report the wall above the entrance was decorated with a mosaic depicting the adoration of the wise men, and the Persians, recognizing in the picture the national dress and insignia of their magi, were so stricken with awe that they did not dare lay hands on the building.[4] Under Mohammedan rule the basilica suffered much damage and neglect at various times, but was never destroyed. Apart from repairs and additions made in different centuries, the original structure is still preserved. The official name of the church is "St. Mary of the Nativity."

Underneath the sanctuary of the basilica is the grotto of the Nativity, the final goal of devout pilgrims throughout the centuries. Originally the cave was fairly spacious and formed several recesses. In one of these was the crib. St. Jerome asserts that it was made of "hardened clay." That would indicate a limestone crib hollowed out of the side of the wall and lined with clay. Cribs of this type are still in use in Palestine.[5]

The whole cave has now been transformed into a crypt chapel. The ceiling is natural, the ground and the walls are made of white Italian marble and decorated with precious ornaments, and many lamps burn day and night. The spot where according to ancient tradition Christ was born, is marked with a silver star in a circle of reddish stone, and surrounding it are the words, *"Hic de Maria Virgine, Jesus Christus natus est"* (Here Jesus Christ was born of the Virgin Mary).

The Firstborn Son · The Gospel narrates that Mary brought forth her "firstborn" son. The word "firstborn" here does not have a numerical meaning as if He were the first of several children, but refers to the legal status of every male Israelite who was the first (or only) child of his parents. According to the Law the firstborn son (in Hebrew, *bekor*) had to be presented in the temple and redeemed by a sacrifice, since he belonged to God according to the ancient Covenant. He was consequently entered in the records as the "firstborn," although he might be the only child the couple ever had. Because of the misunderstanding as to just what "firstborn" meant many made use of it to deny the virginity of Mary, claiming she had other children, though today serious scholars admit such reasoning to be erroneous. The fact that the Jews called their son "firstborn" even when he was the only child, has recently been confirmed by the discovery of a tomb in Egypt, dating from the year 5 B.C. (about the time of Christ's birth). The inscription on this tomb pictures a Jewish mother saying she died in the birth-pangs of her "first-

21

born" son.[6] She could not very well have had more children if she died at the birth of her "firstborn." X

The Song of the Angels · The expression "good will" in the Gospel does not primarily mean the good will of men toward God or each other, but the good will of God toward men, that is, His love, benevolence, kindness, and mercy. The exact sense therefore is, "and on earth peace to men possessing Divine good will."

The English version of the angels' song varies according to different readings in the early Greek manuscripts. It all depends on one single "*s*" (*eudokia* or *eudokias*: "good will" or "of good will"). Most scholars favor the form *eudokias*. On it are based the translations of the Latin (Vulgate), the Syriac, Coptic, and Gothic texts, as well as the Latin Fathers of the Church. The Vulgate is the official text in the Catholic Church. It reads in English translation:

> Glory to God in the highest,
> and peace on earth among men of good will.

The other reading (*eudokia*) is found in some Greek manuscripts and has been widespread in the Eastern churches. It came into English literature through the translators of the King James Bible, and has been generally used by most churches among the English-speaking nations. It reads in English:

Glory to God on high
and peace on earth!
Good will to men!

In late years many scholars—for scientific reasons—have returned to the so-called "Catholic" version (*eudokias*). The Revised Standard Version (Protestant) of the New Testament reads: "on earth peace among men with whom he [God] is pleased." [7]

The Adoration of the Shepherds · Pictures of the Nativity often represent Mary as holding the Child in her arms while the shepherds enter. This scene does not correspond with the text. The Gospel clearly says that the shepherds found Mary and Joseph, "and the babe lying in the manger." Moreover, the angel had announced to them as a special sign that the Child would be found *lying* in the manger.

When Mary is represented holding her Child while the shepherds adore, it is because pious imagination has adorned the Gospel report with added details, picturing her taking the Infant from the crib after the shepherds had found Him, holding Him in her arms while they worship. But more accurately at the moment of the shepherds' approach the Infant should be pictured as lying in the crib. The best representation of this scene seems to be Baroccio's *Nativity*. He places the manger against the wall, and, it would appear, carved out of the rock. Mary kneels adoring before the

23

crib while St. Joseph stands at the door and motions the shepherds to enter.

The Gospel does not report that the shepherds brought presents to the Christ Child. This detail, so often expressed and described in our Christmas stories and pictures, is also an addition to the text and was probably inspired by the love and affection of devout people everywhere from early centuries up to the present day.

The Magi · The name "magi" is not a Hebrew word but of Indo-Germanic origin, meaning "great, illustrious." St. Matthew mentions the term without explanation because it was well known to the people of Palestine. The Magi originated in Media (Persia) and their caste later spread to other oriental countries. They were a highly esteemed class of priestly scholars, devoting themselves not only to religion but also to the study of natural sciences, medicine, mathematics, astronomy, and astrology. In several countries they were members of the king's council.

Quite early in the Christian era a popular tradition conferred on the Magi of Bethlehem the title of kings. This tradition became universal at the end of the sixth century. It was based on Biblical prophecies which described the conversion of the pagans and, although not referring to the Magi, was applied to their visit, as, for instance, in the following texts:

24

The kings of Tharsis and the islands shall offer presents: the kings of the Arabians and of Saba shall bring gifts. —Psalm 71, 10.

The kings shall walk in the brightness of thy rising. . . . They all shall come from Saba, bringing gold and frankincense.—Isaias 60, 3-6.

Where did the Magi come from? St. Matthew gives a general answer: "Wise men from the East." Was it Persia or Arabia? Speaking in modern terms, it could have been any one of the countries of Arabia, Iraq, Iran, Afghanistan, or India. It has never been exactly determined from which of these countries they came.

Neither has their exact number ever been established. The Gospel does not tell us how many they were. The Christians in the Orient had a tradition of twelve Magi. In early paintings and mosaics they are represented as two, three, four and even more. In the occidental church a slowly spreading tradition put their number at three. This tradition became universal in the sixth century. It does not seem to have any historical foundation but was probably based on the fact of the threefold presents which the Magi offered. Another reason for the number three was the early legend that they were representing all humanity in the three great races of Sem, Cham, and Japhet. This particular legend is also the reason for picturing one of the three as a member of the black race.

The book *Collectanea et Flores,* ascribed to St. Bede the Venerable (735), records an early legend of their names and appearance: "The first was called Melchior; he was an old man, with white hair and long beard; he offered gold to the Lord as to his king. The second, Gaspar by name, young, beardless, of ruddy hue, offered to Jesus his gift of incense, the homage due to Divinity. The third, of black complexion, with heavy beard, was called Baltasar; the myrrh he held in his hands prefigured the death of the Son of man." [8]

There is an old legend that when many years had passed the Magi were visited by St. Thomas the Apostle, who after instructing them in Christianity, baptized them. They were then ordained to the priesthood and later made bishops. It is said that once more the star of Bethlehem appeared to them—reunited them toward the end of their lives. "The city of Sewa in the Orient" is given as the place of their burial. [9] The legendary relics of the Magi were brought to Constantinople in the fifth century; one hundred years later they were transferred to Milan, and in 1164 to Cologne under Emperor Barbarossa (1190). Their shrine in Cologne was, and still is, the center of many pilgrimages.

The Massacre of Bethlehem · King Herod (4 B.C.) is considered one of the cruelest tyrants in history. In the course of his reign, it is reported, he drowned his brother-in-law, a youth of sixteen, who was High Priest of Israel; he killed his uncle Joseph, his wife Mariamne, and his mother-in-law Alexandra. His brother-in-law, Kostobar, together with several members of his family, was killed by his order. A few years before the birth of Christ, Herod murdered his two sons Alexander and Aristobulus, and had three hundred officials slain whom he accused of siding with the two young men. In the year 4 B.C., only five days before his death, he had his firstborn son Antipater executed. And when he realized that his own death would probably be greeted with joy and relief by the populace, he brought hundreds of the most illustrious Jews together at Jericho and ordered his servants to kill them all as soon as he died, hoping in this way to make certain there would be tears and mourning in Israel when he was buried. Fortunately, this mad order was not carried out.

Herod like all tyrants killed thousands of innocent people whom he suspected of plotting against him. He was so suspicious of his own subjects and terrified at the thought of rebellion that he ordered the people by special decrees to keep busy at all times. He forbade them to meet together, to walk or eat in groups, and he had his spies everywhere, both in the city and rural districts, watching every move of the citizens. Public and private executions of countless victims took place in his citadel of Hyrcania (overlooking the Dead Sea).[10]

This is the man, St. Matthew reports, who "sent and slew all the boys in Bethlehem and its neighborhood

27

who were two years and under" (2, 16). How many children were killed? At times their number has been wildly exaggerated, as hundreds, even thousands. An approximate figure might be estimated, however, because at the time of Christ, Bethlehem was a small town or village. Assuming a population of two thousand souls, the number of boys of two years and under might be around thirty. Most modern scholars consider even this figure too high and put the number at fifteen or twenty victims. (This slaughter is now commemorated on the Feast of the Holy Innocents.)

The Names of Christmas · The original Latin names for Christmas are: *Festum Nativitatis Domini Nostri Jesu Christi* (The Feast of the Nativity of Our Lord Jesus Christ) and the shorter form, *Dies Natalis Domini* (The Birthday of Our Lord).

From these Latin names most nations derive their popular terms for the Christmas Feast: *Il Natale* in Italy, *La Navidad* in Spain, *Natal* in Portugal, *Nadal* in Southern France, *Nadolig* in Wales (and probably the Gaelic *Nollaig* as well). The Greek *Genethlia* means "Nativity," as do the names for Christmas in Hungarian (*Karácsony*) and in most of the Slavic languages: *Boze Narodzenie* (God's birth) in Polish; *Rozhdestvo Khrista* (Christ's Birth) in Russian and Ukrainian.

The French word *Noel* can be explained as either coming from the Latin *Natalis* (birthday) or from the

28

word *Nowell* which means "news." In an old English Christmas verse the angel says:

> I come from hevin to tell
> The best nowellis that ever befell.

It is possible that both explanations are right. Noel and Nowell may be words of different origin which have become identical in meaning because they are pronounced the same.

The German word for Christmas is *Weihnacht* or (in the plural form) *Weihnachten,* which means "the blessed (or holy) night." Similar terms meaning "the holy night" are used in some Slavic languages (Czech, Slovak, Jugoslavian). The Lithuanian word *Kaledos* is derived from the verb *kaledoti* (to beg, to pray) and has the meaning, "Day of Prayer."

The English word "Christmas" is based on the same pattern as the old names for other feast days in the liturgical year like Michaelmas, Martinmas, Candlemas, and so on. The first mention of the name, *"Cristes Maesse,"* dates from the year 1038. It means "the Mass of Christ." The English nation (as did all Christian nations at the time) acknowledged the sacrifice of the Mass as the most important part of the Christmas celebration. For instance, the word in the Dutch language was *Kersmis* (the Mass of Christ); the old Dutch form is *Kerstes-misse* or *Kersmisse.*

The origin of the word "Yule" is disputed. Some

29

scholars say it comes from the old Germanic word *Iol* (*Iul, Giul,* etc.), meaning a turning wheel (in this instance the sun-wheel rising after the winter solstice). A better explanation, however, might be the Anglo-Saxon word *geol* (feast). Since the greatest popular feast in pre-Christian times was the celebration of the winter solstice, the whole month of December was called *geola* (feast-month). This name was preserved in the English and German languages, and later applied to the feast of Christmas: "Yule" in English, and *Jul* in German.

What is the original meaning of our popular greeting, "Merry Christmas"? When this greeting was originally used, the word "merry" did not mean "joyful, hilarious, gay," as it does today. In those days it meant "blessed, peaceful, pleasant," expressing spiritual joys rather than earthly happiness. It was thus used in the famous phrase, "Merry England."

The well-known carol, "God rest you merry, gentlemen," is an excellent example of the original meaning of "merry." The position of the comma clearly shows the true meaning (that the word is not an adjective describing "gentlemen"), and therefore is not, "God rest you, joyful gentlemen," but, "God rest you peacefully, gentlemen."

CHAPTER 2

Origin of the Feast

There is no record in history, nor even any well-founded tradition, which gives the date of the Saviour's birth. How, then, was December twenty-fifth chosen as Christmas day? It was a common belief among the early Christians of the West that the Nativity took place on the twenty-fifth day of the month; but the exact month was quite uncertain. And so, for the first three centuries, the celebration of Christmas was assigned to various days of the year.

In most places there was no special feast of the Nativity, but the commemoration of the Saviour's birth used to be included in the feast of the Epiphany (Manifestations) on January sixth, one of the oldest annual feasts.

31

There are, however, a few indications from the early centuries that a special religious feast was celebrated, at least in some places, in honor of the Nativity. But there is no mention at all of any popular celebration. After all the early Christians would not very well have had a "Christmas" in their homes when their religion was persecuted and they were forced to hide in the catacombs. They loved and honored the Divine Child heroically, often suffering a martyr's death.

Soon after the end of the last great persecution, however, about the year 320, the Church in Rome definitely assigned December twenty-fifth for the celebration of the birth of Christ. For a while, many Eastern churches continued to keep other dates, but toward the end of the fourth century the Roman custom became universal. The Church did not, of course, rule that we know the precise date of Christ's birth, but merely assigned a certain day in order to unify the celebration of a religious feast of such importance. The fact that December twenty-fifth was chosen, does not seem to rest so much on historical findings, as in the great desire to replace the popular pagan celebration of the winter solstice by the festivities of a truly Christian holiday.

Since about A.D. 400 the whole Christian world has celebrated Christmas on December twenty-fifth, with the exception of the Greek churches, where it is celebrated thirteen days after that date because they did not accept the Gregorian calendar. (Gregory XIII, in 1582, corrected the old Julian calendar—established by Julius Caesar in 40 B.C.—which by that time was ten days behind the actual time schedule. He not only eliminated these ten days but provided for future accuracy by a simple but ingenious arrangement of leap years. The Greek churches, which follow the old Julian calendar, are still thirteen days behind our dates.)

The old Romans celebrated a pagan feast on December twenty-fifth which they called the "Birthday of the Unconquered Sun" (*Natalis Solis Invicti*). This was a feast of the Mithras cult in honor of the Sun-god, celebrating the winter solstice. Consequently, it has been said that the Nativity is only a "Christianized pagan festival." But all Christians during this period were keenly aware of the difference between the two celebrations—one pagan and one Christian—on the same day. In fact, the Popes seem rather to have chosen December twenty-fifth precisely for the purpose of inspiring the people to turn from the worship of a material sun to the adoration of Christ the Lord. This thought seems to be indicated in the writings of contemporary Fathers of the Church. St. Cyprian (258) wrote the beautiful words: "O, how wonderfully acted Divine Providence that on the day on which the Sun was born (solstice) . . . Christ should be born!" [11] St. John Chrysostom (407) exclaimed in one of his books: "They (the pagans) call December twenty-fifth the

33

Birthday of the Unconquered: Who is indeed so unconquered as our Lord? . . . or, if they say that it is
the birthday of the Sun: *He* is the Sun of Justice." [12]

Some Christians, who thoughtlessly retained external
symbols of the Sun-worship on Christmas day, were
immediately and sternly reproved by their religious
superiors and those abuses were suppressed. Proof of
this are the many examples of such warnings in the
writings of Tertullian (third century) and the Christian authors of the fourth and fifth centuries, especially
the sermons of Pope St. Leo I (461) and St. Augustine
(430).

The error of confusing Yule (solstice) and Christmas
(the "Mass of Christ"), as if both celebrations had a
common origin, occurs even in our time. Expressions
like "Christmas originated four thousand years ago" or
"the pagan origins of Christmas" and similar mislead-
ing phrases have only added to the confusion.

While it is certainly true that some popular features
and symbols of our Christmas celebration had their
origin in pre-Christian Yuletide customs, Christmas itself—the feast, its meaning and message—is in no way
connected with any pagan mythology or Yule rite.

The celebration of *three Masses* on Christmas day
(the first traditionally held at midnight), is an old
custom founded in the fifth century by the Church.
The three Masses were celebrated in Rome with great
solemnity; the first at the Chapel of the Manger in the

34

church of St. Mary Major; the second in the church of St. Anastasia (which served as court chapel for the officials of the Emperor who resided at Constantinople); the third in St. Peter's. At this third Mass, on Christmas day A.D. 800, Pope Leo III crowned Charles the Great and proclaimed the new Christian (Roman) Empire of the West.

Christmas soon became a feast of such great importance that from the fifth to the tenth century it marked the beginning of the ecclesiastical year.

The Emperor Theodosius, in 425, forbade the cruel circus games on Christmas day, and Emperor Justinian, in 529, prohibited work and public business, declaring Christmas a civic holiday. The council of Agde (506) urged all Christians to receive Holy Communion on Christmas day. The council of Tours (567) proclaimed the twelve days from Christmas to Epiphany as a sacred and festive season, and established the duty of Advent fasting in preparation for the feast. The council of Braga (563) forbade fasting on Christmas day.

Thus the groundwork was laid for a joyful celebration of the Lord's Nativity, not only in the house of God, but also in the hearts and homes of the people.

CHAPTER 3

Christmas in the Middle Ages

The great religious pioneers and missionaries who brought Christianity to the pagan tribes of Europe, also introduced the celebration of Christmas. It came to Ireland through St. Patrick (493), to England through St. Augustine of Canterbury (604), to Germany through St. Boniface (754). The Irish monks, St. Columban (615) and St. Gall (646), introduced it into Switzerland and Western Austria; the Scandinavians received it through St. Ansgar (865). To the Slavic tribes it was brought by their apostles, the brothers St. Cyril (869) and St. Methodius (995); to Hungary by St. Adalbert (997).

Most of these Saints were the first bishops of the countries they converted and as such they established and regulated the celebration of the Nativity. In England, St. Augustine observed it with great solemnity. On Christmas day, 598, he baptized more than ten thousand Britons. In Germany, the observance of Christmas festivities was officially regulated by a synod in Mainz in 813.

About the year 1100, all the nations of Europe had accepted Christianity, and Christmas was celebrated everywhere with great devotion and joy. The period from the twelfth to the sixteenth century was the peak of a general Christian celebration of the Nativity, not only in churches and monasteries, but in every home as well. It was a time of inspiring and colorful religious services. Carols and Christmas plays were written. It was at this period, too, that the many delightful Christmas customs of each country were introduced. Some have since died out; others have changed slightly through the ages; many have survived to our day. A few practices had to be suppressed as being improper and scandalous, such as the custom of dancing and mumming in church, the "Boy Bishop's Feast," the "Feast of the Ass," New Year's fires, superstitious (pagan) meals, impersonations of the devil, irreverent carols, and similar abuses.

It was during the period from 1100 to 1500 that a large number of popular practices, legends, and superstitions developed. For example: At midnight on Christmas, it was thought that a mysterious universal celebration took place in nature, that a spirit of peace and adoration prevailed over the whole world. The cattle in the stables fell on their knees; so also the deer in the forest. This legend found its way into the New World through the French in Canada, who spread it among the Indians. Harrison in his *Sketches of Upper Canada* relates how at midnight one Christmas eve he met an Indian creeping cautiously along in the stillness of the woods. The Indian, upon seeing him, motioned him to be silent, and when asked for the reason, replied that he was out to watch the deer kneel because he believed that on Christmas night all deer would fall on their knees to the Great Spirit and adore.[13]

Similar legends relate that the bees awake from sleep and hum a beautiful symphony of praise to the Divine Child; but only those can hear it who are dear to the Lord. In the Orient there is a legend that during the holy night all trees and plants, especially those on the banks of the Jordan, bow in reverence to the Saviour. The birds sing all night at Christmas; their voices become sweeter and more melodious, even the sparrows sound like nightingales. A Lithuanian legend relates how on Christmas eve the water in wells and fountains is blessed by God with great healing powers and heavenly sweetness. Mysterious bells are heard pealing joyously during the holy night from the depths of deserted mines, and cheerful lights may be seen blinking at the bottom of lonely shafts and caves.

One of the oldest Christian legends is the charming story related by St. Gregory of Tours (594) in his *Libri Miraculorum* (Book of Miracles) concerning the Well of the Magi near Bethlehem. The people of Bethlehem made a practice of going there during Christmas week, bending over the opening of the well and covering themselves and the opening with blankets or cloaks, to shut out the light of day. Then, as they peered into the dark well, the star of Bethlehem, according to this pious practice, could be seen moving slowly across the water—but only by those who were pure of heart.[14]

Other legends tell of how animals could talk like humans at midnight. Their favorite language seemed to be Latin. In an old French mystery play the cock crows with a piercing voice, *"Christus natus est"* (Christ is born): the ox moos *"Ubi?"* (Where?): the lamb answers *"Bethlehem,"* and the ass brays *"Eamus!"* (Let us go!).[15] In the Austrian Tyrol the animals in the stable are said to gossip about the public and hidden faults of those who listen in on their conversation. In Lithuania, the cattle and sheep and horses compare notes as to how they were treated by their masters during the past year.

It was a widespread practice to be especially kind to animals at Christmas and to allow them to share in the joy of the Feast. As you may have already guessed,

39

this custom was begun by St. Francis of Assisi (1226). He admonished the farmers to give their oxen and asses extra corn and hay at Christmas, "for reverence of the Son of God, whom on such a night the blessed Virgin Mary did lay down in the stall between the ox and the ass." All creation, said he, should rejoice at Christmas, and the dumb creatures had no other means of doing so than by enjoying more comfort and better food. "If I could see the Emperor," he said, "I would implore him to issue a general decree that all people who are able to do so, shall throw grain and corn upon the streets, so that on this great feast day the birds might have enough to eat, especially our sisters, the larks." [16]

According to the counsel of this lovable Saint, new straw was put in the stables at Christmas, more and better food was given to beasts, the wild birds were fed with corn, and all domestic animals were granted a time of rest from hard work during the twelve days of the holy season.

Another legend inspired the popular belief that the power of malignant spirits, of ghosts and witches, was entirely suspended during the Christmas season. The mystical presence of the Christ Child made them powerless; no harm could be done to men, or beasts, or homes. Shakespeare has made this legend immortal by these familiar lines:

40

Some say that ever 'gainst that season comes
Wherein our Saviour's birth is celebrated,
The bird of dawning singeth all night long:
And then, they say, no spirits dare stir abroad;
The nights are wholesome; then no planets strike,
No fairy takes, no witch has power to charm,
So hallowed and so gracious is the time.[17]

A very old and practical superstition made it obligatory on Christmas eve to see that the house was thoroughly cleaned, all borrowed articles returned, all tools laid aside, no lint allowed "to remain on rock or wheel," no unfinished work exposed to sight, and no task started which could not be finished by nightfall.

It was an old and comforting belief among the Irish people that the gates of Paradise were open Christmas at midnight, so that any person dying at that hour could enter Heaven at once. Another legend considered every child born at Christmas especially blessed and fortunate. In addition to other gifts and privileges, such children were said to have the power of seeing spirits, and even of commanding them.

Finally there is the lovely medieval legend of the "Christmas Angel." Every year—so the story goes—the blessed Virgin Mary selects a number of angels and sends them out from Heaven into various parts of the world. Each angel awakens a little child from its first sleep and carries it to Paradise to sing a carol to the Christ Child. When the children afterwards tell of their

41

beautiful errand, some people will say it was just a dream; but those who know better will assure you that these children are chosen by God to be blessed with unusual favors in this life and with great glory in the next.

CHAPTER 4

Decline and Revival

With the Reformation in the sixteenth century there naturally came a sharp change in the Christmas celebration for many countries in Europe. The sacrifice of the Mass—the very soul of the Feast—was suppressed. The Holy Eucharist, the liturgy of the Divine Office, the sacramentals and ceremonies all disappeared. Gone were the colorful and inspiring processions, the veneration of the blessed Virgin Mary and the Saints. All this was ridiculed and forbidden as a "popish superstition."

In many countries all that remained of the once rich and glorious religious festival was a sermon and a prayer service on Christmas day. Although the people

43

kept many of their customs alive, the deep religious inspiration was missing, and consequently the "new" Christmas turned more and more into a pagan feast of good-natured reveling.

On the other hand, some sects including the German Lutherans preserved a tender devotion to the Christ Child and celebrated Christmas in a deeply spiritual way within their churches, hearts, and homes.

In England, however, the Puritans condemned even the reduced religious celebration which was held in the Anglican Church after the separation from Rome. They were determined to abolish Christmas altogether, both as a religious and as a popular feast. It was their contention that no feast of human institution should ever outrank the "sabbath" (Sunday); and as Christmas was the most important of the non-Sunday festivals, they directed against it all their attacks of fierce indignation. Pamphlets were published denouncing Christmas as pagan and its observance was declared to be sinful. In this anti-Christmas campaign these English sects were much encouraged by the example of similar groups in Scotland, where the celebration of the Feast was forbidden as early as 1583, and punishment inflicted on all persons observing it.

When the Puritans came to political power in England, they immediately proceeded to outlaw Christmas. The year 1642 saw the first ordinances issued forbidding church services and civic festivities on Christmas day. In 1644, the monthly day of fast and penance was appointed for December twenty-fifth. The people, however, paid scant attention to these orders and continued their celebrations. There was thus inaugurated a great campaign of two years' duration (1645-1647). Speeches, pamphlets and other publications, sermons and discussions were directed against the celebration of Christmas, calling it "antichrist-Mass, idolatry, abomination," and similar names. Following this barrage of propaganda, the Parliament ordained on June 3, 1647, that the feast of Christmas (and other holidays) should no longer be observed under pain of punishment. On December 24, 1652, an act of Parliament again reminded the public that "no observance shall be had on the five-and-twentieth of December, commonly called Christmas day; nor any solemnity used or exercised in churches in respect thereof." [18]

Each year, by order of Parliament, the town criers went through the streets a few days before Christmas, reminding their fellow-citizens that "Christmas day and all other superstitious festivals" should not be observed, that market should be kept and the stores remain open on December twenty-fifth.

During the year 1647 popular riots broke out in various places against the law suppressing Christmas, especially in London, Oxford, Ipswich, Canterbury, and the whole county of Kent. In Oxford there was a "world of skull-breaking"; in Ipswich the festival was

45

celebrated "with some loss of life"; in Canterbury "the mob mauled the mayor, broke all his windows as well as his bones, and put fire to his doorsteps." [19] An ominous note was sounded against the republican Commonwealth at a meeting of ten thousand men from Kent and Canterbury, who passed a solemn resolution that, "if they could not have their Christmas day, they would have the King back on his throne again." [20]

The government however stood firm and proceeded to break up Christmas celebrations by force of arms. People were arrested in many instances but were not punished beyond a few hours in jail. Anglican ministers who decorated their churches and held service on Christmas day, were removed from their posts and replaced by men of softer fiber.[21] Slowly, and relentlessly, the external observance of Christmas was extinguished. December twenty-fifth became a common work-day, and business went on as usual. But in spite of these repressive measures many people still celebrated the day with festive meals and merriment in the privacy of their homes.

When the old Christmas eventually returned with the restoration of the Monarchy (1660), it was actually a "new" Christmas. The fine old traditions of religious observance so close to the hearts of all Christians today had disappeared from the homes of England. What was left was a worldly, shallow feast, of amusements and reveling. Instead of the old carols in praise of the

Child of Bethlehem, the English people observed Christmas with rollicking songs in praise of "plum pudding, goose, capon, minced pie and roast beef." [22] An excellent example of this new attitude is contained in a Christmas song from *Poor Robin's Almanack* (1695):

> Now thrice welcome Christmas,
> Which brings us good cheer,
> Minc'd pies and plum-porridge,
> Good ale and strong beer;
> With pig, goose and capon,
> The best that may be,
> So well does the weather
> And our stomachs agree.
> Observe how the chimneys
> Do smoke all about,
> The cooks are providing
> For dinner no doubt. . . .

Two famous descriptions of this new kind of "Christmas without Christ," are found in Charles Dickens's *Christmas Stories* and in Washington Irving's *Sketch Book*. These are typical of many individual Christmas celebrations in our own time, though even in these substitutions for a feast, once so deeply religious, the spirit of good will to all and of generosity to the poor prevails.

The Irish people for centuries were deprived of their beloved ancient Christmas customs through religious and political persecutions. Yet they are an outstanding

47

example of a people who kept the very soul of Christmas alive through the ages, finally bringing it to new lands and sharing it with people of all faiths.

The unfortunate and misdirected zeal against Christmas persisted in America, far into the nineteenth century. In New England, it is hard to realize now, Christmas was outlawed until the second half of the last century. Our Pilgrim fathers, for instance, worked as usual on their first Christmas day in America, although they observed the most rigid Sabbath-rest on the preceding day, which was Sunday. Governor Bradford noted that "no man rested all day" on December 25, 1620. December twenty-fifth until 1856 was a common work-day in Boston, and those who refused to go to work on Christmas day were often dismissed. In New England today there are many who remember their grandparents telling them that in some instances factory owners would change the starting hours on Christmas day to five o'clock or some equally early hour in order that workers who wanted to attend a church service would have to forego, or be dismissed for being late for work. As late as 1870, classes were held in the public schools of Boston on Christmas day and any pupil who stayed at home to observe the Feast was gravely punished, even shamed by public dismissal.

It was not until the Irish and German immigrants arrived in large numbers toward the middle of last century that Christmas in America began to flourish as it does today. The Germans brought their beloved Christmas tree. They were soon joined by the Irish, who contributed the ancient Gaelic custom of putting lights in the windows. Both groups, of course, brought the crib, or crèche, their native carols and hymns, the three Masses on Christmas day, and the religious obligation of attending Mass and abstaining from work on the feast of the Nativity.

Very soon their neighbors, charmed by these unusual but attractive innovations, followed their example and made many of these customs their own. For some years, however, many clergymen continued to warn their congregations against celebrating Christmas with these "new" customs. But eventually a powerful surge of enthusiasm from people of all faiths swept resistance away. New Englanders especially were so won over by this friendly, charming way of celebrating Christmas that a revival of deeper and richer observance followed in many of their churches. One by one, the best of the old traditions were lovingly studied, revived, and became again common practice. Catholics and Protestants cooperated, uniting in a sincere effort to restore the beauties of a truly Christian celebration of the Nativity.

The Latin countries, many nations of Central Europe, especially the rural sections of southern Germany and Poland, the Alpine provinces of Austria, and Bavaria, have been especially loyal to ancient Christmas customs, blending charmingly the traditions of medieval times with the best of modern Christmas customs. In commemoration of the legend that tells how the birds and beasts of the field came to worship the infant Jesus, the young Polish peasants dress up as various creatures such as the stork and the bear and go from house to house singing the traditional carols. They are paid with gifts of food. Many celebrations which have disappeared or lost their meaning elsewhere may still be found in these countries in their original purity.

CHAPTER 5

The Midnight Mass

Mass is said at midnight on Christmas because it is generally believed that Christ was born at that hour. There is, of course, no historical evidence to uphold this pious belief, which has its source in the following reference to Christ's birth in the Book of Wisdom (18, 14-15):

For while all things were in quiet silence, and the night was in the midst of her course, Thy almighty word leapt down from heaven from Thy royal throne, as a fierce conqueror into the midst of the land of destruction.

As the context shows, these words refer to the slaying of the firstborn in Egypt; but the medieval theologians

51

applied it as a prophetical reference to the Incarnation of the Divine Word. A beautiful Latin hymn of the fourth century (*Quando noctis medium*) expresses this common belief of our Lord's birth at midnight:

> When the midnight, dark and still,
> Wrapped in silence vale and hill:
> God the Son, through Virgin's birth,
> Following the Father's will,
> Started life as Man on earth.

Midnight has never been assigned as the official time for the first Mass. It is merely prescribed that it be said *"in nocte"* (during the night). Hence in many places the first Mass is celebrated before dawn, at four or five in the morning. During the early centuries (400-1200) the Roman regulations prescribed that the first Mass should be celebrated *"ad galli cantum"* (when the cock crows), which was about three o'clock in the morning.[23] A relic of this custom is found among the Spanish-speaking people, who even today call the midnight Mass *"Misa de Gallo"* (Mass of the cock).

Among the French people it is an old custom to hold a joyful family gathering and a traditional meal (*réveillon*) directly after midnight Mass. In Spain people promenade on the streets after the midnight Mass with torches, tambourines, and guitars, singing and greeting each other. In some parts of Germany the figure of the Christ Child is solemnly placed in the crib after the first Mass, while the people in church sing their ancient carols.

In the church of the Nativity in Bethlehem, the statue of the Divine Child is placed on the altar after the first Mass and then carried in procession to the crypt, where it is laid on the silver star which marks what is believed to be the actual spot of the Lord's birth. The Gospel of St. Luke is sung, and when the Deacon comes to the words, "she laid him in a manger," the statue is lifted from the floor and placed in the rock-hewn crib next to the star.

Another custom connected with midnight Mass is the ringing of church bells during the solemn service of "Vespers," which is held in many places directly before the midnight service. In America, chimes and carillons accompany or replace the bells in many churches, ringing out the tunes of familiar carols, especially the joyous invitation, "O come, all ye Faithful."

In Austria, Bavaria, and other countries of Central Europe, carols are played from the church towers before midnight Mass; the tunes of traditional Christmas songs ring out through the stillness of the winter night, clear and peaceful, creating an unforgettable impression.

In some sections of England, Ireland, and Scotland, a quaint and unusually interesting custom was practiced in medieval times. One hour before midnight the big bell of the church would begin to toll its slow and solemn message of mourning, and it would thus continue for the whole hour, as if tolling for a funeral. But at the moment of midnight, just as the clock struck twelve, all the bells would suddenly ring out in a merry peal of Christmas joy. This tolling from eleven to twelve was called "the devil's funeral," for according to the old legend, the devil died when Christ was born.

CHAPTER 6

Ancient Hymns and Carols

The word "carol" comes from the Greek word *choraulein* (*choros:* the dance, *aulein:* to play the flute), and referred to a dance accompanied by the playing of flutes. Such dancing—usually done in ring form—was very popular in ancient times among the Greek and Roman people. The Romans brought the custom and its name to Britain.

In medieval England "carol" meant a ring-dance accompanied by singing. The dancers would form a circle and, joining their hands, walk in rhythmic dance-step while keeping the form of the circle (as our

55

children still do in their "ring-around-a-rosy" game). Chaucer describes such a ring-dance in his *Romaunt of the Rose* (lines 798-804), using the word "carol" for the dance itself. He pictures himself approaching a group of dancing young ladies, and one of them "ful curteisly" calls him:

> "What do ye there, beau sire?" quod she;
> "Come neer, and if it lyke yow
> To dauncen, daunceth with us now."
> And I, withoute tarying,
> Wente into the caroling.

Gradually the meaning of "carol" changed, and the word was applied to the song itself. In an English-Latin vocabulary of 1440 a synonym for carol would be "song, psalmodium."

A hymn is essentially solemn; a carol, in the modern sense, is familiar, playful or festive, but always simple. The distinction between hymns and carols is often overlooked and "carol" has come to denote all vernacular songs pertaining to Christmas.

The first hymns in honor of the Nativity were written in the fifth century, soon after Christmas was fully established as one of the great annual feasts. These hymns, written in Latin, increased in number as time went on. Some of them were incorporated in the Divine Office and are still used at Christmas time in the daily prayers of the breviary, while still others are sung by church choirs at liturgical services. Many Latin hymns (1200-1700) were translated into various languages and have since become popular carols.

The early Latin hymns (400-1200) are profound and solemn, and dwell exclusively on the supernatural aspects of Christmas. Theological in text, they do not concern themselves with the human side of the Nativity. A few of the best known early Latin hymns are:

Jesus refulsit omnium (Jesus, Light of all the nations), by St. Hilary of Poitiers (368).

Corde natus ex Parentis (Of the Father's love begotten), by Prudentius (405), a layman, government official of the Roman Empire, and great Christian poet.

Agnoscat omne saeculum (Let every age and nation know), by Venantius Fortunatus (602), Bishop of Poitiers.

A song of the ancient Greek Church which in English translation still survives is the hymn, "O gladsome Light" (*Phos hilaron*); it is used in many churches at Christmas candlelight services.

Other Latin hymns which were later translated and became popular carols were:

In hoc anni circulo (In the circle of this year)
Dies est laetitiae (O royal day of holy joy)
Flos e radice Jesse (A spotless rose is growing); this hymn of the sixteenth century was set to music, in its present familiar tune, by Michael Praetorius (1621), a German priest.

57

The birthplace of the true Christmas carol was Italy. There, in the thirteenth century among the early Franciscans, St. Francis of Assisi was the first to introduce the joyous carol spirit which soon spread all over Europe. He had a particular devotion and affection for the mysteries of the holy childhood of Jesus. His biographer, Thomas of Celano (about 1260), says, "The Child Jesus was forgotten by the hearts of many. But with the grace of God He was resurrected again and recalled to loving memory in those hearts through His servant, the Blessed Francis." [24]

St. Francis wrote a beautiful Christmas hymn in Latin (*Psalmus in Nativitate*), but there is no evidence that he composed carols in Italian. His companions and spiritual sons, however, the first Franciscan friars, contributed a large number of lovely Italian Christmas carols. Here is an English translation of one of these thirteenth century Italian carols. The tune has become very familiar as the theme on which Handel developed his Pastoral Symphony in the *Messiah*:

> In Bethlehem is born the Holy Child,
> On hay and straw in the winter wild;
> O, my heart is full of mirth
> At Jesus' birth.

From Italy the carol spread quickly to Spain and France, and finally all over Europe. In Germany in the fourteenth century a great many popular Christmas carols were written largely under the inspiration of the Dominican mystics, John Eckhardt (1327), John Tauler (1361), and Blessed Henry Suso (1366).

The earliest known English carol was written at the beginning of the fifteenth century. It is a lullaby of great simplicity and tenderness:

> I saw a sweet, a seemly sight,
> A blissful bird, a blossom bright,
> That mourning made and mirth among;
> A maiden mother meek and mild
> In cradle keep a knave child   (knave: boy)
> That softly slept; she sat and sung:
>> Lullay, lulla, balow,
>> My bairn, sleep softly now.

These early English carols usually employed both rhyme and alliteration. There followed a great number of English Christmas poems in the next two centuries, most of them very tender and devout, praising the Divine Child and His Virgin Mother.

> Blessed be that lady bright
> Who bare a child of great might
> Without pain, as it was right,
>> Maid, Mother Mary.

 → to page 81

CHAPTER 7

Carols for Every Mood

Christmas carols may be divided into many groups and appealing classifications, such as nativity carols, prayer carols, mystery carols, and so on. To list all of them would fill a volume, but here are a few excellent examples for various moods.

Nativity Carols · This, the largest group, is made up of Christmas carols in the strict sense of the word, the main theme being the story of the Nativity itself. They reveal the religious feeling which the birth of Christ brings to the hearts of men and usually express adoration, praise, love, gratitude, contrition, wonder, joy, and similar emotions, like this ancient English carol:

A child is born in Bethlehem;
Rejoice, therefore, Jerusalem.
Low in the manger lieth He,
Whose kingdom without end shall be. . . .
All glory, Lord, to Thee be done,
Now seen in flesh, the Virgin's Son.

A solemn note announcing the wondrous news is
sounded in the simple hymn "God Eternal" (*Boh Pre-
dvichniy*), a traditional carol of the Ukrainian people:

God Eternal was born.
From heaven He came;
All His people to save
Was He kindly pleased.

In Bethlehem was He born,
Our Christ and our Lord,

And Master of us all:
For us was He born.

In contrast is one of the old Spanish (Catalan) carols expressing the joy of Christmas in a festive manner (the word *foom* is an imitation of the humming sound of guitars and mandolins):

Many feasts the good Lord gave us,
Sing: foom, foom, foom.

Summer feasts are better, though;
    But let us praise Him even so:
For He does our needs remember
    And sent us Christmas in December.
Foom, foom, foom.
On December twenty-fifth,
    Sing: foom, foom, foom.
A little child was born that night,
    So sweet and small, at dawn of light.
Dark was the stable, cold and bare,
    When blessed Mary bore Him there.
Foom, foom, foom.

The opposite sentiment—compassion and sweet sadness—is expressed in a traditional Slovak carol:

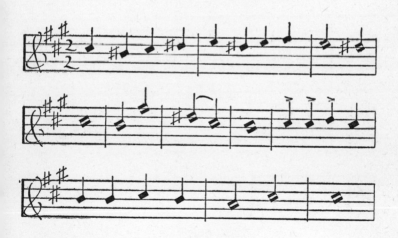

It was a night in winter,
    Man and beast asleep,

When Jesus, poor and humble,
    Did His vigil keep.
The Lord whom kings and prophets
    Lovingly foretold,
Lies trembling in a stable,
    Dark and bitter cold.
Is this the only welcome,
    Saviour, at Thy birth?
Is loneliness and sadness
    All you find on earth?

Prayer Carols · An excellent example of these Christmas songs directly addressed to the Holy Child in wonder and admiration is the Austrian children's carol, *Lied der Kinder zu Bethlehem* (Carol of the Children of Bethlehem):

Thou hast come, O Saviour dear,
To redeem us; Thou art here:
Mother told me so.

Cold and freezing is the night,
But Thy love is warm and bright
Like the fire's glow.

Poor, O Jesus, is Thy home,
Winds through all the corners roam;
I would not stay here!

Leave the stable and the hay,
Come with me to live and play!
Won't you, Jesus dear?

Another beautiful prayer carol is the poem *Tu scendi dalle stelle* (Thou camest from the Heavens), written by Pope Pius IX (1878) and sung to a traditional melody:

> Thou camest down, O heaven's King,
>   From starry sky,
> And in a cave so poor and cold
>   I see Thee lie.
> I see Thee tremble, blessed God;
>   Why should this be?
> Thy sacrifice, O love Divine,
>   Is all for me.

Mystery Carols · These carols form a large group of medieval Christmas songs delightfully describing all manner of legendary events supposed to have happened to the Divine Child. One of the most charming English mystery carols is the following old song: [25]

> As Joseph was a-walking,
>   He heard an angel sing:
> This night shall be born
>   Our heavenly king.
>
> He neither shall be born
>   In housen or in hall,
> Nor in the place of Paradise,
>   But in an ox's stall.
>
> He neither shall be clothed
>   In purple nor in pall,

65

But all in fair linen,
As were babies all.

He neither shall be rock'd
In silver nor in gold
But in a wooden cradle
That rocks on the mould.

Shepherd Carols · These songs flourished in Germany, Austria, England, France, Ireland, Italy, Spain, as well as in the Slavic nations. They relate the message of the angel, the song of the heavenly hosts, the visit of the shepherds to the manger, and often describe their prayers and gifts. Many of these carols carry refrains imitating shepherds' instruments; for instance this merry English carol of the fifteenth century:

About the field they piped full right,
Even about the midst of the night;
They saw come down from heaven a light:
Tirlè, tirlè—so merrily
The shepherds began to blow.

In another early English carol, the last shepherd in a group, after presenting a cap as his gift, speaks this humble prayer:

This gift, Son, I bring thee is but small,
And though I come the hindmost of all,
When Thou shall them to Thy blisse call:
Good Lord, yet think on me!

Many carols invite the shepherds to hurry and adore the new-born Lord, as in this Austrian shepherds' carol:

> Rise, shepherds, though the night is deep,
>   Rise from your slumber's dreaming!
> Jesus, the Shepherd, watch does keep,
>   In love all men redeeming.
> Hasten to Mary and look for her Child,
>   Come, shepherds, and greet our Saviour mild!

Noels · The Noels are still another group of carols, of which we have many examples both in French and in English. The word "Noel" or "Nowell" is generally repeated as a refrain, in the sense of "news." Who does not know the familiar carol "The first Noel"? It has become a favorite Christmas song among all English-speaking people. As an example of the Noel refrain, we quote the closing lines of another ancient English carol:

> Noel, noel, noel,
> Noel sing all we may,
> Because the King of all kings
> Was born this blessed day.

Macaronics · A macaronic is a carol written partly in Latin, partly in the vernacular. There are many of these in French, English, and German. Here is an English macaronic of the sixteenth century:

> Now make us joy in this feste
> In quo Christus natus est,

67

A Patre unigenitus. . . .
Sing to Him and say welcum,
Veni Redemptor gentium.

Lullaby Carols · These songs, as the classification suggests, make use of the lullabies of various countries, either picturing the Virgin Mary singing to the Holy Child or having the devout worshiper sing them directly to the Divine Babe, like this old Austrian carol:

Thy shining eyes, so blue and light,
Thy tender cheeks, so soft and bright;
I will remain forever Thine,
O dearest Son, O child Divine. . . .
(lullaby humming)

A quaint old carol sung by the nuns at St. Mary's Abbey, Chester, England, is a combination of an old Latin hymn (*Qui creavit caelum*), with a lullaby verse after each line. The earliest manuscript of this macaronic dates from the beginning of the fifteenth century:

The Lord who created the heavens,
  Lully lully lu;
Is born in a stable,
  Byby byby by,
The King of all mankind,
  Lully lully lu.
Between two animals
  Byby byby by,

Lies the Joy of the world,
Lully lully lu,
Sweet beyond anything,
Byby byby by.[26]

Again there is the endearing Czech lullaby so typical of many similar songs among the Slavic nations. It is impossible to render in English the charming spirit of the original Czech text:

Hajej, nynej, Jesus dear,
Sleep in peace, and do not fear.

69

We shall bundle you to rest,
    Keep you close to our breast.
Hajej, nynej, darling Child,
    Son of Mary, Saviour mild.

Companion Carols · This is an extremely interesting group of songs—mostly German—wherein the singer represents himself as accompanying the shepherds, or as taking their place, addressing the Child, or Mary and Joseph, in a simple, affectionate manner. Often a broad local dialect is used, as in the old Austrian carol from the Tyrol, *Jetzt hat sich halt aufgetan das himmlische Tor* (The gates of heaven's glory did spring open suddenly). Here is a rollicking, joyous stanza:

So came we running to the crib,
    I and also you,
A bee-line into Bethlehem,
    Hopsa, trala loo:
"O, baby dear, take anything
    Of all the little gifts we bring:
Have apples or have butter,
    Maybe pears or yellow cheese;
Or would you rather have some nuts,
    Or plums, or what you please.
Alleluja, alleluja;
    Alle-, alle-, Alleluja."

Another lively companion carol is the *Weihnachtslied der Jäger* (Hunters' Carol) from Austria:

Awake, O drowsy hunters,
  Hear the whistles and the horn!
Get up from lazy slumber,
  For our Saviour Christ is born.
From the trumpets' jolly playing
  Let the hills and valleys ring,
Hark, the hunting hounds are baying;
  Go and greet the new-born King!
Awake from sleep, O hunters:
  It is the morn of Christmas day.
(*Hunting horns*): Tri-di-ay-ho-di-ay-ho-dio. . . .

Dance Carols · Dance carols, usually ring-dances accompanied by singing, were greatly favored in medieval times. The altar boys, for example, in the Cathedral of Seville, Spain, used to dance before the altar on Christmas and other feast days, accompanied by song and the sound of castanets. In the Minster of York, England, until the end of the sixteenth century, choir boys performed a dance in the aisle of the church after morning prayers on Christmas day. In France it was customary to dance a *bergette* (shepherd's dance) in churches at Christmas time. Dancing in churches was prohibited by an ecclesiastical council at Toledo in 590, but the custom had become so much a part of the Christmas festivities that in some places dancing survived until the thirteenth and fourteenth century, and, in England, right up to the Reformation (in Spain even longer).

71

A famous old English carol from a mystery play pictures Christ as announcing the mystical marriage to His "true love"—the Church—and narrating His acts of love to her:

> Tomorrow shall be my dancing day,
>   I would my true love did so chance
> To see the legend of my play,
>   To call my true love to my dance.
> Sing, oh! my love, oh! my love;
>   This have I done for my true love.
>
> In a manger laid and wrapp'd I was,
>   So very poor, this was my chance,
> Betwixt an ox and a silly poor ass,
>   To call my true love to my dance.
> Sing, oh! my love, oh! my love;
>   This have I done for my true love.

Christmas dancing is still practiced in the Scandinavian countries, where carols are sung as the people perform a ring-dance around the Christmas tree. A popular dance carol is the Swedish *Nu ar det Jul igen* (Now it is Christmas again):

Now Christmas is here again,
　And Christmas is here again,
　　And Christmas we'll have till Easter.
Then Easter is here again,
　And Easter is here again,
　　And Easter we'll have till Christmas.
Now this will not be so,
　And this will not be so,
　　For in between comes Lenten fasting.

A traditional Austrian carol invites the shepherds and the faithful to dance before the crib:

Bring your pipes and bring your drum,
　Call the shepherds all to come;
Hasten quick, no time to lose,
　Don't forget your dancing shoes.
Frolic we right merrily:
　He will laugh with happy glee,
Yes, and smile, and we will dance,
　While He claps His tiny hands.

Jesus dearest, Thee to greet,
　Hasten we with dancing feet.
When the time will come to die,
　In Thine arms we beg to lie.

All our sins forgive, we pray,
  Miserere Domine.
Grant us then with Thee to dwell,
  In heaven's bliss, Emmanuel.

Epiphany Carols · These carols tell the story of the three Magi, their journey to Bethlehem, the adoration, the presents offered, and other details, including sentiments of prayer and devotion. Many of them are like ballads and of considerable length. Here is the beginning of an old English Epiphany carol:

Three kings came out of Indian land
  To see the wondrous Infant bent,
With rich presents in their hand;
  Straightly a star before them went.
A wondrous thing it was to see:
  That star was more than other three. . . .

⚹ An Epiphany song of deep devotion is the old Portuguese carol *Os Reis* (The Kings):

Out of the Orient they came ariding
  Three noble kings, of humble heart and mild;
They came to see the Blessed Lord of Heaven
  Descend to earth, to be a little child.
Precious gifts of gold and myrrh and incense,
  Bringing God the gifts which God had made:
Low the kings in homage bowing,
  At the feet of Mary laid.

Cradle-Rocking · This word comes from the German *Kindelwiegen* (Rocking of the Child), a custom which originated in Germany and Austria in the fourteenth century. It became widespread as a substitute for the Nativity plays, after they were banned. A priest would carry to the altar a cradle with a figure of the Christ Child; there the cradle was rocked while the congregation sang and prayed. The service ended with the devotional kissing of the Christ Child at the altar rail.

During the sixteenth century this custom, too, was forbidden in churches, but it survived for a long time as a devotional practice in many convents and in private homes. In the Tyrol, girls dressed in white carried the cradle from house to house, rocking it and singing carols. In other parts of Austria, and in Bavaria, mothers would rock the cradle to obtain the favor of having children, or to implore the Divine Child for special blessings upon their families. The rocking was accompanied by songs written for this particular purpose, for instance, this German carol of the sixteenth century:

> Joseph, dearest Joseph mine,
> Help me rock my baby fine!
> What Gabriel foretold
> Is now fulfilled,
> Eia, Eia,
> The Virgin bore a child

As the Father's wisdom willed.
Eia, Eia.
Joseph, dearest Joseph mine,
Help me rock my baby fine!

Star Carols · These songs are sung by young people who go from house to house at Epiphany, carrying a pole with the "Star of Bethlehem," and impersonating the Magi, reporting the adventures of their journey and wishing all a happy and holy Christmas. This custom, a simplified form of the ancient Epiphany plays, was widespread in England, Holland, France, Austria, and Germany from the end of the fourteenth century until the Reformation. It is still practiced in Austria, Bavaria (*Sternsingen*), and the Slavic countries.

We are the three Kings with our star,
We bring you a story from lands afar:
And so, dear people, we say to you—
It might sound strange, but is really true—
That something happened in the Holy Land;
We went there, all three, by God's command,
And in Bethlehem's stable we found a child:
Our new-born Saviour, sweet and mild. . . .

Christmas Yodeling · Christmas yodeling is an old custom in the Austrian Tyrol, where it seems a natural way to honor the Divine Child. The mountaineers' song without words conveys deep feelings of devotion, love, and affection. This is, of course, the genuine yodel, not the modern hillbilly type so familiar to American radio fans. True Christmas yodeling is capable of great tenderness of voice and melody as the subtle changes from chest tones to head tones are delicately made by the yodelers.

They do this before the crib or in the open on mountain peaks during the holy season. It was performed in the churches during past centuries. Some yodels are based on old traditional tunes; others are improvised on the spur of the moment. Often the yodeling forms a background as Christmas carols are sung.

Here is an old yodel-carol from the Austrian Tyrol in which singing and yodeling alternate; the singing is done by two groups: men (representing the shepherds) and women (representing the angels):

To Christ our Lord we raise this song,
    (*Yodel*): Hol-di-ah-di-ay.
Chimes are ringing, angels singing,
    (*Yodel*): Hol-di-ah-di-ay.

The Cherubim and Seraphim
Pour out their songs in praise of Him:
    (*Angels*): Amen.

Oh, look here! No, look there!
Angels' choirs everywhere:
    (*Yodel*): Hol-di-ah-di-ay.
    (*Angels*): Alleluja.

Those fortunate enough to have experienced a Tyrolean Christmas are forever haunted by the beauty and simplicity of these voices coming out of the mountains.

CHAPTER 8

Familiar Hymns and Carols

After the Reformation most of the old hymns and carols were no longer sung, and consequently forgotten in many countries, until their revival in the nineteenth century.

Christmas carols in general were discouraged by the Calvinists, who substituted metrical psalms in their place. Carol singing was altogether suppressed by the Puritans, for instance. Following the restoration of Christmas in England, however, there were numerous festive songs in praise of the Feast, but very few religious carols. One of the few, however, that has become a favorite among English-speaking nations is the ballad, "While shepherds watched their flocks by night," written by Nahum Tate (1715). Its familiar music was taken from the "Christmas melody" of Handel's opera *Siroe*, and arranged in the present setting by Richard Storrs Willis, in 1850.

Even as late as 1823, an English collector of Christmas lore, William Hone (1842), wrote in his *Ancient Mysteries* that carols were considered as "something past," and had no place in the nineteenth century. The Methodist revival in the eighteenth century, however, had inspired a number of modern hymns, first used only in Methodist churches, but gradually welcomed among all English-speaking people. The best-known of these is "Hark, the herald angels sing," written by Charles Wesley. The music was adapted from Mendelssohn's *Festgesang* (written in 1840) by William H. Cummings, organist at Waltham Abbey, England, in 1885.

Another popular English "carol" of the last century is the song "Good King Wenceslaus." This is not a Christmas carol in the strict sense, but rather the poetic story of a famous miracle ascribed in medieval legend to St. Wenceslaus, Martyr, Duke of Bohemia (935). The miracle, according to the poem, occurred "on the day of Stephen" (December twenty-sixth), and thus became one of the English Christmas carols. The tune was originally a sixteenth century spring canticle and the words were written by John M. Neale (1866).

The carol "Joy to the world! The Lord is come,"

came from the pen of an English poet, Isaac Watts (1748). Lowell Mason (1872) of Medfield, Massachusetts, composed the music from tunes found in Handel's *Messiah*. This carol first appeared in print in 1839 and has become one of America's favorites.

The Lutherans in Germany wrote new hymns for their own use. Among these are some of the best modern carols, such as Martin Luther's delightful song, *Vom Himmel hoch da komm' ich her* (From heaven above I come to you), which he wrote in 1535. Bach composed a harmonization for it in his *Christmas Oratorio*.

Another carol ascribed to Martin Luther, and widely used in America, is the beautiful "Away in a manger." It is usually called "Luther's cradle hymn," though the words and music were not written by him. It might very well have been inspired, however, by the second part of the first stanza of Luther's hymn *Vom Himmel kam der Engel Schar*, which starts with the line, *"Ein Kindlein zart, das liegt dort in der Krippen"* (Away there in the manger a little Infant lies). The familiar English text is of American origin, very likely written in one of the settlements of German Lutherans in Pennsylvania. The poem appeared in print in Philadelphia, 1885. Since then, forty-one settings have been written for this carol; the most popular ones are the tunes composed by James R. Murray (who, erroneously, ascribed the authorship of the poem to Luther) in 1887, and by William James Kirkpatrick (1921).

Within the past two centuries a number of excellent carols have been written in Germany, many being adopted as popular church hymns. Some have become favorite songs in other countries. The best-known of these are:

O du fröhliche . . . (O, thou joyful Christmas time), a popular carol, written by Johann Falk in 1816. The tune was taken from an old Sicilian Madonna-hymn in Latin, *O Sanctissima.*

O Tannenbaum (O Christmas Tree), an early nineteenth century carol, is familiar in this country as the tune to which the words of *Maryland, My Maryland* are set.

Ihr Kinderlein, kommet (O come, all ye children), written by Christoph von Schmid (1854) and sung to a tune composed by Johann A. P. Schulz (1800), has become the favorite children's carol in Germany and is now frequently heard in churches in this country.

The first American carol was written by the famous missionary of the Huron Indians, saint and martyr, John de Brebeuf, S.J. (1649), who labored among the Hurons from 1626 until he was captured and slowly tortured to death by the savage Iroquois who brutally attacked and destroyed the Huron mission in 1649 and 1650.

Father Brebeuf wrote in the Huron language the Christmas hymn *Jesous Ahatonnia* (Jesus is born), which he adapted from a sixteenth century French folk song. This hymn was preserved by the Hurons who escaped the devastating attacks of the Iroquois and were later settled by their missionaries in a reservation at Loretto, near Quebec. There Father Étienne de Villeneuve recorded the words of the hymn; they were found among his papers after his death (1794) and later published with a French translation.

In recent years Brebeuf's hymn has been re-introduced into the treasury of American Christmas carols. J. E. Middleton, of Toronto, wrote a free English translation to fit the ancient French melody. The music was arranged by Edith Lovell Thomas, music director at the church in Radburn, New Jersey. Here is the second stanza of Brebeuf's hymn in the original Huron language and the English translation. (The Hurons have no *M*. Whenever it occurred in foreign words, the missionaries substituted for it the French diphthong *ou*, as in the name of the Blessed Virgin, which was written "Ouarie" and pronounced "Warie" as in the first word of the third line in the following Huron text.)

> Aloki ekwatatennonten shekwachiendaen
> Iontonk ontatiande ndio sen tsatonnharonnion
> Ouarie onnawakueton ndio sen tsatonnharonnion
>   Iesous ahatonnia!
>
> O, harken to the angels' word,
>   Do not decline

To heed the message which you heard:
   The Child Divine,
As they proclaim, has come this morn
Of Mary pure. Let us adore.
   Jesus is born.

A great number of beautiful American carols were introduced in the last century, inspired not only by the Methodist revival but also as a result of the widespread renascence of Christmas customs. These American carols are quite different from the average English Christmas songs during the past centuries because they reflect a religious spirit, while most early English carols praise only the external pleasures of feasting, reveling, and general good will, without direct reference to the Nativity of Christ.

"It came upon the midnight clear" was written by Edmund H. Sears (1876), a Unitarian minister of Weston, Massachusetts, and set to music by Richard S. Willis (1900), a journalist and editor in Detroit (in his youth, a personal friend of Mendelssohn).

One of the most beloved of American carols is the famous "O little town of Bethlehem" written by Phillips Brooks (1893), well-known former rector of Trinity church (Episcopal) in Boston, and later Episcopal Bishop of Massachusetts. He visited the Holy Land, and the impression made on him by the Christ Child's birthplace inspired him to write this poem three years

84

after his return to Holy Trinity church in Philadelphia, in 1865, where he was then stationed. Louis H. Redner (1908), the organist there and teacher in the church school, wrote the tune. It was first sung by the children of Holy Trinity Sunday school, on Christmas 1868.

"We three kings of Orient are" was written and set to music in 1857, by John Henry Hopkins Jr. (1891), an Episcopalian minister. It was published in 1883 and has been popular with children ever since.

Another famous American carol is Henry Wadsworth Longfellow's poem entitled "Christmas Bells" ("I heard the bells on Christmas Day"). He wrote it for Christmas 1863, and the poem reflects the horrors of the Civil War which had afflicted his own family, his son, a lieutenant in the army, having been seriously wounded.

> Then from each black, accursed mouth
> The cannon thundered in the South,
>   And with the sound
>   The carols drowned
> Of peace on earth, good will to men!
>
> And in despair I bowed my head:
> "There is no peace on earth," I said,
>   "For hate is strong
>   And mocks the song
> Of peace on earth, good will to men!"
>
> Then pealed the bells more loud and deep:
> "God is not dead, nor doth He sleep!

> The Wrong shall fail,
> The Right prevail,
> With peace on earth, good will to men!"

The tune used for Longfellow's poem is called "Waltham" and was composed by the English organist, John Baptist Calkin (1905).

Other familiar carols in this country include: "Angels we have heard on high," most probably a translation of an old French or Flemish antiphon-hymn of the sixteenth century. (An antiphon-hymn is a free poetic translation, in the vernacular, of one or more antiphon verses in liturgical texts, like the Divine Office of the breviary, or the texts used in the Mass and at Vespers.) This particular hymn was probably inspired by the antiphons of the Lauds in the Divine Office of Christmas day. The present version of the English text was written by Earl Marlatt, Dean of the School of Theology at Boston University, in 1937; the arrangement for the "Gloria" was made by Edward Shippen Barnes, in 1937.

A startling example of nineteenth century American folk-music from the Kentucky mountains, is the song, "Christ was born in Bethlehem, and Mary was his niece." Another popular one, "The snow lay on the ground," is of uncertain origin. The melody was taken from an old Italian *pifferari* (pipers') melody. One of the favorites among many Negro contributions to

American Christmas music is "Rise up, shepherd, an' foller."

The well-known Christmas song "O Holy Night" is of French origin. Adolphe Charles Adam (1856), Professor at the Paris Conservatory of Music, wrote the tune to a poem (*Cantique de Noël*) of M. Cappeau de Roquemaure. The English translation was made by John Sullivan Dwight (1893).

Despite the devoted research of musical scholars the origin of the beloved Christmas hymn *Adeste Fideles* (O Come, All Ye Faithful) is still shrouded in mystery. The original Latin poem is sometimes ascribed to St. Bonaventure (1274), a Franciscan priest, later Archbishop and Cardinal. However, the original manuscripts, containing text and tune, date from the eighteenth century and are signed by John Francis Wade (1786), a music dealer of the English Catholic colony at Douay, France. Marcus Antonius de Fonseca (Portogallo), chapelmaster to the king of Portugal (1830), has also been mentioned as composer of the music. This tune is reported to have been sung at the Portuguese embassy chapel in London, at the end of the eighteenth century. Dr. Frederick Oakely (1880), an Anglican minister and later Catholic priest, wrote the English version of the text in 1841.

More recent contributions include *Gesu Bambino*, words by Frederick Marten and music by Pietro Yon (1943), organist and choir-master of St. Patrick's Cathedral in New York; it is contrapuntal, in the pastoral manner, against the *Adeste Fideles* melody. Another favorite is "The world's desire" by G. K. Chesterton.

In Austria—especially its Alpine provinces—many parishes had, and some still retain, their local poets who continue to add new songs to the old treasury. In little towns and on the farms of the Alpine sections, men and women of "singing families," and the rural choirs are continually improvising words and music like minstrels of old. These simple folk have a native instinct for music and poetry. Many of them play instruments (violin, flute, zither, guitar), and improvise Christmas songs as they gather round the hearth. Any student of Christmas lore will find in Austria and Bavaria a rich treasury of popular carols, ancient and modern, hidden away in little country places. Most of them as yet are unknown to the world in general, though the famous Trapp singers have brought many of them to this country and they are now included in many Christmas programs here.

One such familiar Austrian carol, written by a parish priest in the small town of Oberndorf, near Salzburg, in 1818, is the familiar *Stille Nacht, Heilige Nacht* (Silent Night, Holy Night). It had been hidden among the manuscripts of the church choir for some time, until it was found by a music-lover who brought it to the Rainers, a family of singers, in the Tyrol (*Zillertal*). They began to sing it at their concerts and it gradually became widely used in Austria and Germany. On their American concert tour (1839-1843) they brought the new carol with them and sang it before large audiences.[27] Within a few years it conquered the hearts of the nation. Not only in America but all over the world "Silent Night" has become the most beloved of all carols, a truly international Christmas anthem.

Here is the story of its origin: On Christmas eve, 1818, the parish priest of Oberndorf, Joseph Mohr, was notified that repairs of the church organ (which had broken down a few days before) could not be finished in time for midnight Mass. This was a great disappointment to the priest and his flock, since the music for the High Mass which the choir had prepared could not be sung. To lessen the disappointment, Father Mohr decided to surprise his people with a new Christmas song. He went to work immediately and wrote three stanzas of a carol, the first stanza of which was inspired by the sight of a baby whose ailing mother he had visited earlier in the day. Having finished the text, he brought it to his friend, Franz Gruber, teacher and organist in the nearby village of Arnsdorf. Gruber composed the tune within a few hours. At midnight Mass, the hushed congregation in the little church heard the first performance of *Stille Nacht*.

Today a modest monument in Oberndorf perpetuates the memory of the men who gave us "Silent

Night": the priest-poet, Joseph Mohr (1848), and the composer, Franz Gruber (1863).

Stille Nacht was first performed to the accompaniment of a guitar. The composer later wrote an orchestration for strings, French horn, and organ. Father Mohr called it *Weihnachtslied* (Christmas song). It was first published at Leipzig, in 1834. The commonly used English translation appeared in a Methodist hymnal in Boston, in 1871, and had been compiled from various preceding translations. (The name of the compiler is unknown.)

In Latin countries, especially in rural sections of Spain and South America, many towns have their traditional Christmas carols which have now become part of American Christmas lore in certain sections of the country. These are carols of childlike simplicity, often humorous in parts, but always devout and tender. The local carol of the town Ocumare de la Costa (Venezuela), a jewel of popular Christmas music, is a good illustration (*El Niño Jesús ha nacido ya*):

The little child Jesus is already here,
The Kings and the shepherds adore without fear.
There is much to behold for the wise and the fool:
Saint Joseph, the Virgin; the ox and the mule.
    Let us adore the little child
    With pleasure and happy cheer;
    Let us adore as the Magi do
    As the Magi adore Him here.[28]

The first mention of Christmas caroling in America
is recorded by Father Bartholomew Vimont, S.J., in his
report on the state of the Huron mission, dated Quebec,
October 1, 1645. In it he described the zeal and
devotion which the Christian Hurons displayed in celebrating Christmas. Speaking of the Indians at Mackinac (now Mackinaw, Michigan), one of the most remote missions of New France, he says: "The savages
have a particular devotion for the night that was en-
lightened by the birth of the Son of God. There was
not one who refused to fast on the day that preceded

91

it. They built a small chapel of cedar and fir branches in honor of the manger of the infant Jesus. They wished to perform some penance for better receiving Him into their hearts on that holy day, and even those who were at a distance of two days' journey met at a given place to *sing hymns in honor of the new-born Child*. . . . Neither the inconvenience of the snow nor the severity of the cold could stifle the ardor of their devotion." [29]

This ancient custom of singing carols in public was revived in America at the beginning of this century. In Boston, the first organized Christmas eve caroling took place on the streets of Beacon Hill in 1908 and continues to this day, many families holding open house. In St. Louis it was started in 1909 by groups of young people who sang their carols before every house with a lighted candle in its windows. Organized groups of carol-singers may now be found in thousands of American cities and towns.

In French Canada, the caroling is performed either a few days before Christmas or on New Year's eve, by young men and women dressed in old-style country costumes (*La guignolée*), who go from house to house, singing and collecting gifts of food and clothes for the poor of the town.

In Hungary, in Poland, and other Slavic countries singers go from house to house carrying a huge star, lighted inside. After their carols are sung, some of the groups enact scenes from the Nativity, the visit of the

Magi, the court of King Herod, etc.; this custom is called *Kolednicy* in Polish, *Bethlehem* in Hungarian. National groups in this country have done much to preserve some of these customs during the holiday season. Again, it would fill a small volume to include all of them.

CHAPTER 9

Nativity Plays

In the early centuries, the story of the Nativity was dramatized in churches within the framework of so-called "miracle plays." These semi-dramatic services consisted in pious representations of the "mystery" of Christ's birth, accompanied by song, prayer, and other acts of devotion. (Mystery, in this connection, is the religious term for any episode of Christ's life related in the Gospels.) In those days, of course, books or pictures were not available to most of the common people, so these plays served not only as acts of worship but also as a means of religious instruction. They soon became very popular in all Christian countries. A typical Nativity play given in the Cathedral of Rouen

(France) in the twelfth century may be described in this way:

Behind a curtain, in the sanctuary of the church, a picture of Mary with the Child was placed in an enclosure representing the stable of Bethlehem. A procession of the canons of the cathedral, vested in tunics and impersonating the shepherds, entered the church through the main door. Inside the church the procession halted while a choir boy from the gallery above announced to them the Nativity in the words of the angel. The canons responded singing, *"Eamus usque Bethlehem"* (Let us go to Bethlehem) and proceeded through the main aisle toward the altar reciting the hymn, *Pax in terris nunciatur.* As they passed through the gate of the sanctuary, a boys' choir began to sing *"Gloria in excelsis Deo"* (Glory to God in the highest), to which the priests answered, *"Et in terra pax hominibus bonae voluntatis"* (and on earth peace to men of good will).

Within the sanctuary two other priests in dalmatics met them, inquiring: *"Quem quaeritis?"* (Whom do you seek?). They answered, *"Salvatorem qui est Christus Dominus"* (Our Saviour who is Christ the Lord). The two priests then drew back the curtain and sang, *"Adest hic parvulus cum Maria Matre sua . . . Alleluia"* (The little Child is here with Mary his mother . . . Alleluia); and pointing to the picture of Mary they added, *"Ecce Virgo"* (Behold the Virgin).

95

The priests, proceeding to the enclosure, bowed reverently, venerated the Child, and saluted the mother with prayer and songs. Then singing "Alleluia" they returned in procession to their choir stalls. Immediately following this dialogue, midnight Mass was celebrated.[30]

There is a touching note of childlike piety and devotion in these early church plays, revealing the deeply religious manner in which plays were used to help in Divine service. From such beginnings grew that bewildering number of mystery plays which flourished in all parts of Europe from the eleventh to the fifteenth century. As time went on the plays became more elaborate and covered more details of the Biblical story. Fictional and legendary scenes were added and the congregation was allowed to take part.

As a natural but unfortunate result of these changes, many abuses appeared such as irreverence, comedy, improper behavior of clergy and laymen, sensational effects, and similar aberrations. The authorities of the Church protested against such scandal; but things had gone too far for correction and change. Under the pretext of tradition the warnings and admonitions of the Bishops were ignored or neglected. After all efforts had failed to restore the church plays to their original character, the whole institution was gradually suppressed and finally forbidden during the fourteenth and fifteenth centuries and miracle plays were no longer performed in churches.

This banishment, however, brought about an indirect blessing. In order to survive outside the church, the plays were purged of their abuses and were able now to employ many dramatic effects that formerly had been impossible in church plays. There subsequently developed a rich growth of religious drama which flourished up to the Reformation and continued to flourish long after in many countries. The schools of the Jesuit Fathers were centers of this dramatic movement until the order was suppressed (1773).[31]

The restoration of Christmas customs in the last century also brought about a revival of Nativity plays—not dramatic performances of the long and tiresome seventeenth and eighteenth century "morality plays," but simple, devotional plays of the earlier type. In fact, these old plays, in simplified form and with certain restrictions, had never ceased to exist in some sections of Germany and Austria, even in churches.

It was from Germany that the Nativity pageant found its way into America. As far as is known, the first such play in this country was performed in the German Catholic church of the Holy Trinity in Boston, Massachusetts, Christmas, 1851.[32] The children of the parish, dressed as Oriental shepherds, carrying bundles of food, linen, and other gifts, proceeded in solemn procession to the crib in front of the altar, singing Christ-

97

mas carols. They honored the Divine Child by offering their presents, reciting prayers and chanting hymns. The parish priest accepted the offerings, which were afterwards distributed to the poor. The children in their Oriental costumes, their hands folded devoutly, left the church in a street procession after the service. This performance attracted such attention and admiration from people of all faiths in Boston that it had to be repeated twice during Christmas week upon the urgent request of both Catholics and Protestants from all over the city who were anxious to witness this "new pageant, so charming, so edifying." This procession at Holy Trinity Church, Boston, has been held every year since then, though of late in simplified form without costumes.

Gradually the Nativity plays became a cherished part of American Christmas celebrations in both Catholic and Protestant church halls, in many of their organizations and societies, and more recently in public schools. These modern Christmas plays are without exception short, simple in structure, deeply devout and reverent in character, like the Nativity plays created a thousand years ago.

A peculiar type of Nativity play is the German *Herbergsuchen* (Search for an inn). It is a dramatic rendition of the Holy Family's fruitless efforts to find a shelter in Bethlehem. Joseph and Mary, tired and weary, knock at door after door, humbly asking for a place to stay. Realizing that they are poor, the owners refuse their request with harsh words, until they finally decide to seek shelter in a stable.

Usually the whole performance is sung and often it is followed by a "happy ending" showing a tableau of the cave with the Nativity scene. There are scores of different versions according to the various songs and sketches provided in the text. Here is one stanza of a traditional Austrian *Herbergsuchen* (*Wer klopfet an?*):

> Who's knocking at my door?
>> Two people, poor and low.
> What are you asking for?
>> That you may mercy show;
> We are, oh sir, in sorry plight,
> O grant us shelter here tonight.
> You ask in vain.
>> We beg a place to rest—
> It's "no" again!
>> You will be greatly blessed.
> I told you, no! You cannot stay,
> Get out of here, and go your way!

A similar custom is the Spanish *Posada* (the Inn), traditional in South American countries, especially Mexico. On an evening between December sixteenth and twenty-fourth, several neighboring families gather in one house where they prepare a shrine, handsomely decorated, and beside it a crib with all its traditional

99

figures, but the manger is empty. At night a priest comes to the house, reads prayers and burns incense before the pictures of Mary and Joseph. Then a procession is formed, the two images carried at the head. The group moves through the house, reciting a litany and chanting hymns, until it reaches a room on the top floor where a carol is sung in which St. Joseph begs for a shelter. The people stationed within the room respond, refusing St. Joseph's request as part of the carol. The procession then proceeds to the place where the altar has been prepared. Pictures of Joseph and Mary are put in the shrine, venerated with prayer and incense, and all those present are blessed by the priest. Thus the religious part of the *Posada* ends. Then comes a gay party for the adults consisting of games and refreshments, while the children are entertained with the *Piñata*. This is a fragile clay jar, suspended from the ceiling and filled with candy and other goodies. The object is to break the jar with a stick so the contents spill and everybody rushes pell-mell for some of its treasures.

Another favorite mystery play was the "Office of the Star," a pageant of the Magi's visit on the feast of the Epiphany. Like the Nativity play, this originated as a part of the liturgical service in church (in the eleventh century, probably in France) and soon spread into all European countries. However, from a devout religious ceremony it degenerated into a boisterous affair, due to the appearance of King Herod, who was introduced into the play as a raging maniac, throwing a wooden spear around, beating clergy and laity alike, creating havoc in both sanctuary and church by his antics.

Because of these abuses, the "Office of the Star" was soon abolished as a part of the liturgical service. In its place appeared very early the "Feast of the Star," an Epiphany play performed partly outside the church, partly inside, but in no way connected with the Mass or the liturgical Office. One of the earliest reports of this pageant is in Milan, 1336, where it was directed by the Franciscan friars as an inspiring religious ceremony. The "Three Kings," crowned and richly clad, appeared on horseback with a large retinue, bearing golden cups filled with myrrh, incense, and gold. They rode in state through the streets of the city to the church of St. Eustorgius where they dismounted, entered in solemn procession, and offered their gifts at the Christmas crib.[33]

These Epiphany plays spread quickly through all of Europe; the interest in them was heightened because the Crusaders had brought back tales and Oriental customs from the Holy Land. They were finally prohibited as church plays after the Reformation and completely discarded as religious pageants in many countries, degenerating into wild Dragon plays, "Thre Kynges" puppet shows, and other demonstrations. In more religious communities they kept their original character,

101

somewhat simplified like the *Sternsingen* in Germany and the festival of *Los tres Rejes* (The three kings) among Spanish-speaking nations.

The first description of an Epiphany pageant in America appears in the *Jesuit Relations* of 1679. These Relations are annual reports which the Superiors of the Order at Quebec compiled from letters of the Jesuit missionaries who labored among the Indians of New France (Canada). In the Relation of 1679, there is a delightful report by Father Jean Enjalran, missionary of St. Ignace, a remote outpost of the Canadian Mission on the shores of Lake Huron (now St. Ignace, Michigan). At that time, St. Ignace consisted of a mission station and settlements of various Huron and Algonquin tribes.

In his report Father Enjalran tells of an Epiphany pageant and procession held by the Indians on January 6, 1679. Here is his description, with some minor omissions:

All the savages, but especially the Hurons, professed a special devotion for the all-endearing mystery of the birth of our Lord Jesus Christ. They themselves entreated the priest, long before the feast day, to celebrate it in a most solemn manner. They sent their children to seek materials for constructing a grotto for the Nativity scene. A little girl gathered a beautiful sort of grass, and said that she had done it in the hope that the little infant Jesus might be laid upon that grass.

102

All the Christians went to confession; and those to whom permission was given to receive Holy Communion, did so very devoutly at midnight Mass. The grotto of the Nativity was frequently visited and the Indians exclaimed excitedly and prayed in childlike fashion as they looked on the scene. Then they asked the Father if they might carry the infant Jesus through their village.

They were very anxious to imitate what in other ages had been done by the three strange great Chiefs, who came to adore Jesus Christ in the manger All the Hurons, Christians and non-Christians alike, divided themselves into three companies according to the different clans that made up their village; and, after choosing their chiefs, one for each clan, they furnished them with *wampum* (porcelain), to offer to the infant Jesus. Each one adorned himself as handsomely as he could. Each of the chiefs held a scepter in his hand to which the wampum was fastened, and each wore a gaudy headdress in the form of a crown.

The three companies took up different positions. The sound of a trumpet was the signal for marching. In Indian file the first company started to march, proceeded by a star which was fastened to a large standard of sky-blue color. The second company then demanded the object of their journey; and, on learning it, joined them. The third company followed and all three groups marched into the church, the star remaining at the entrance.

The three chiefs first prostrated themselves and laid their scepters at the feet of the infant Jesus in the cradle. Next they offered their congratulations and presents to the Saviour. They made a public protestation of the submission

103

and obedience which they desired to render Him; asked for the grace of faith for those who possessed it not, and protection for their whole tribe and for all that land; and, in conclusion, entreated Him to approve their bringing Him into the village, where He should be Master.

The priest promised to carry the little statue of the Divine Infant. He now took it from the grotto, out of the cradle, and carried it on a fine linen cloth. Everyone seemed deeply moved, and pressed forward in the crowd, to get a better view of it. The Hurons left the church in the same order in which they had come. The Father walked behind them, carrying the statue, preceded by two Frenchmen who bore a large standard on which was represented the infant Jesus and Mary. All the Algonquins—and especially the Christians, who had been invited to assist—filed solemnly along.

They marched toward the Huron village, chanting the litanies of the Virgin they had been taught and proceeded to a cabin, where they had prepared a lodging for the Infant as appropriate as they could make it. There they offered thanksgiving and prayers.

Afterwards the Child was carried back to the church and replaced in the grotto. The Christian Algonquins were then invited by the Christian Hurons to a feast, at which they exhorted each other to obey Jesus Christ, who was the true Master of the world.[34]

It is hard to realize that all this happened in America as long ago as 1679.

CHAPTER 10

The Christmas Crib

The building of the Christmas crib, or crèche, is a very old custom in most European countries. Within the past century it has been adopted by many different groups and churches in this country. The child in the manger and various other representations of the story of Bethlehem have been used in church services from the first centuries. The earliest known picture is the Nativity scene (about A.D. 380) which served as a wall decoration in the burial chamber of a Christian family, discovered in St. Sebastian's Catacombs, Rome, 1877.

The crib in its present form and its use outside the church is credited to St. Francis of Assisi. He made the Christmas crib popular through his famous cele-

105

bration at Greccio (Italy) on Christmas eve, 1223, with a Bethlehem scene including live animals. His biographer, Thomas de Celano, writes:

It should be recorded and held in reverent memory what Blessed Francis did near the town of Greccio, on the feast day of the Nativity of our Lord Jesus Christ, three years before his glorious death. In that town lived a certain man by the name of John (Messer Giovanni Velitta) who stood in high esteem, and whose life was even better than his reputation. Blessed Francis loved him with a special affection because, being very noble and much honored, he despised the nobility of the flesh and strove after the nobility of the soul.

Blessed Francis often saw this man. He now called him about two weeks before Christmas and said to him: "If you desire that we should celebrate this year's Christmas together at Greccio, go quickly and prepare what I tell you; for I want to enact the memory of the Infant who was born at Bethlehem, and how He was deprived of all the comforts babies enjoy; how He was bedded in the manger on hay, between an ass and an ox. For once I want to see all this with my own eyes." When that good and faithful man had heard this, he departed quickly and prepared in the above mentioned place everything that the Saint had told him.

The joyful day approached. The brethren [Franciscan friars] were called from many communities. The men and women of the neighborhood, as best they could, prepared candles and torches to brighten the night. Finally the Saint of God arrived, found everything prepared, saw it and rejoiced. The crib was made ready, hay was brought, the ox and ass were led to the spot. . . . Greccio became a new Bethlehem. The night was made radiant like the day, filling men and animals with joy. The crowds drew near and rejoiced in the novelty of the celebration. Their voices resounded from the woods, and the rocky cliff echoed the jubilant outburst. As they sang in praise of God the whole night rang with exultation. The Saint of God stood before the crib, overcome with devotion and wondrous joy. A solemn Mass was sung at the crib.

The Saint dressed in deacon's vestments, for a deacon he was [out of humility, St. Francis never became a priest, remaining a deacon all his life], sang the gospel. Then he preached a delightful sermon to the people who stood around him, speaking about the nativity of the poor King and the humble town of Bethlehem. . . . And whenever he mentioned the Child of Bethlehem or the name of Jesus, he seemed to lick his lips as if he would happily taste and swallow the sweetness of that word.[35]

Since the time of St. Francis, the Christmas crib has been a familiar sight in Christian homes all over the world. Farmers in the mountain provinces of Central Europe spend the long winter evenings of Advent repairing and enlarging their beautiful cribs, which are sometimes made up of hundreds of figures, filling a whole room. In many towns of Italy, Germany, and Austria, as well as in South America, there are clubs where children learn to build cribs of various styles and shapes, using their imagination, a veritable manual

107

training course in fashioning a Christmas crib. In Vienna, for instance, there were more than two hundred such cribs, built by boys in one parish, just before World War II. The youngsters were allowed free rein and there were some utterly charming and tenderly fashioned cribs as a result. No two were identical, and there was much originality displayed.

Among the German sects which kept the custom of Christmas cribs even after the Reformation, were the *Herrenhuter,* usually called Moravians. One small group of Moravian missionaries came to America and founded the town of Bethlehem, Pennsylvania, on Christmas eve, 1741. The inhabitants of Bethlehem, and later those of other Moravian settlements in Pennsylvania, brought with them the custom of the crib. They called it "putz" (from the German *putzen:* decorate) and included not only the scene of the Nativity but in addition all the charming details of a German *Krippe* (crib): dozens, sometimes hundreds of figures, fanciful landscaping, waterfalls, houses and fences, bridges, fountains, villages, gardens and groves. The custom of "putzing" and "putz-visiting" has been preserved among them up to this day. It has remained, however, a local practice among German-Americans, especially in Pennsylvania, and has not become a general part of Christmas customs in this country.

The animals in the crib—usually an ass and ox—although not mentioned in the Bible are traditionally now part of the picture. St. Francis was following tradition when he had these animals placed near the manger. As early as the fourth century they were represented in pictures of the Nativity. The custom originated because of two passages in the Old Testament that were applied to the birth of Christ: the words of Isaiah (1, 3), "The ox knoweth his owner, and the ass his master's crib; but Israel hath not known me and my people hath not understood"; and the verse of Habakkuk (3, 2) in the *Itala* version, "In the midst of two animals Thou shalt become known."

One of the most endearing of crib festivities is the famous custom of the Children's Sermon at the church of Ara Coeli on the Capitoline Hill in Rome. (Incidentally, it is said that while standing on the top steps of this church, surveying Rome, the historian Gibbon was inspired to write his *Decline and Fall of the Roman Empire*.) Preserved in this church is a beautiful statue of the Holy Child, carved from wood, wrapped in linen and adorned with a crown. This *Bambino* is highly venerated. (Charles Dickens describes it in his Italian sketches.) All through the Christmas season it lies in the church crib and is visited by thousands. On a platform in front of the crib little boys and girls between five and twelve recite short sermons and poems in honor of the infant Saviour. Adults crowd around and listen with rapt attention as the little ones preach to their elders. Visitors to Rome during the

109

Christmas season count this as one of their most precious experiences because the simplicity of the little Italian children touches their hearts.

On the octave of Epiphany a great procession proceeds from the church of Ara Coeli. The statue of the *Bambino* is borne to the open space at the top of the steps which lead up to the Capitoline Hill, and there the priest, raising the statue high, solemnly blesses the Holy City and all its children.

The Christmas crib was brought to America by many nationalities and is now generally accepted as part of the Christmas celebration in most churches.

CHAPTER 11

Symbolic Lights
and Fires

Those of the Jewish faith annually celebrate in December the anniversary of the Re-dedication of the Temple as a "feast of lights" (Hanukkah). Christians have made the Nativity their feast of lights in honor of Him who was born as a Light to illuminate the nations (Luke 2, 32).

In medieval times it was customary to represent Christ the Lord by a burning candle. This custom is still preserved in the liturgy of the Church, as for instance, the Easter candle, the last candle at the Tenebrae services of Holy Week. At Christmas, a large candle symbolizing the Lord used to be set up in the

111

homes of the faithful on the eve of the Feast. It was placed in the center of a laurel wreath and kept burning through the Holy Night, and was lit, thereafter, every night during the holy season.

The custom of the Christmas candle is still kept in its original form in some countries. In Ireland, the mother or the father of the household lights a holly-bedecked large candle on Christmas eve while the entire family prays for all its dear ones, both living and departed. Among the Slavic nations (Poles, Ukrainians, Russians) the large Christmas candle is put on the table after it has been blessed by the priest in church. The Ukrainians do not use candlesticks but stick the candle in a loaf of bread.

In many sections of South America the candle is placed in a paper lantern with Christmas symbols and pictures of the Nativity decorating its sides. In England and France the Christmas light often consisted of three individual candles molded together at the base, in honor of the holy Trinity. In Germany the Christmas candle used to be placed on top of a wooden pole decorated with evergreens (*Lichtstock*), or sometimes many smaller candles were distributed on the shelves of a wooden structure made in the form of a pyramid, adorned with fir twigs or laurel, draped with glittering tinsel (*Weihnachtspyramide*). (During the seventeenth and eighteenth century this pyramid was replaced by our Christmas tree.)

In addition to the main candle, it later became a custom to set up other smaller candles all through the house in honor of the Feast:

> Then be ye glad, good people,
> This night of all the year,
> And light ye up your candles:
> His Star is shining near.

The custom of placing lighted candles in the windows at Christmas was brought to America by the Irish. The historical background of this custom is interesting. When religion was suppressed throughout Ireland during the English persecution, the people had no churches. Priests hid in forests and caves and secretly visited the farms and homes to say Mass there during the night. It was the dearest wish of every Irish family that at least once in their lifetimes a priest would arrive at Christmas to celebrate the Divine sacrifice during Holy Night. For this grace they hoped and prayed all through the year. When Christmas came, they left their doors unlocked and placed burning candles in the windows so that any priest who happened to be in the vicinity could be welcomed and guided to their home through the dark night. Silently he entered through the unlatched door and was received by the devout with fervent prayers of gratitude and tears of happiness that their home was to become a church during Holy Night.

To justify this practice in the eyes of the English

113

soldiers, the Irish people used to explain: "We burn the candles and keep the doors unlocked, that Mary and Joseph, looking for a place to stay, will find their way to our home and be welcomed with open doors and open hearts." The English authorities, finding this Irish "superstition" harmless, did not bother to suppress it. The candles in the windows have always remained a cherished practice of the Irish, although many of them have long since forgotten the earlier significance. The custom was brought to this country in the early nineteenth century and spread throughout the land, so much so that in recent years electric candles and lights of all kinds are used in homes and in public squares during the Christmas season. Business districts as well as suburban streets spend much time and money to make their decorations gay and bright with lights.

An inspiring and colorful sight are the Christmas fires burned on the peaks of the Alps in Central Europe. Like flaming stars they hang in the dark heavens during Holy Night, burning brightly and silently, as the farmers from around the mountain-sides walk through the winter night down into the valley for midnight Mass. Each person carries a lantern, swinging it to and fro; the night seems alive with hundreds of glow-worms converging toward the great light at the foot of the mountain—the parish church—shining and sparkling, a "Feast of Lights," indeed. No one who has witnessed

114

this scene on Christmas eve in Austria, Bavaria, or Switzerland will ever forget it.

A seasonable Christmas in England and Northern Europe is a cold one. In past centuries it was even colder than it is now because the "old Christmas"— before Pope Gregory XIII corrected the Julian calendar in the sixteenth century—came eleven days later, on January fifth of the present calendar.

At a time when coal and other modern heating fuels were unknown, the firewood to be burned during Holy Night and on Christmas assumed special significance. A huge log was selected and brought to the house with great ceremony in preparation for the ceremony. It was called the "Christmas log" or "Yule log," as Herrick sings:

> Come, bring with a noise,
> My merrie, merrie boyes,
> The Christmas Log to the firing. . . .

In some places the Yule log was the whole trunk of a tree, carefully selected on the preceding feast of Candlemas and stored away to dry out during the summer. Many popular customs and ceremonies were connected with the Christmas log. The unburnt parts, for instance, were put aside and preserved because the new log of next year had to be kindled with wood from the old one. The main purpose of the log, however, was to blaze and burn on the open hearth during Holy Night and on Christmas day.

In spite of modern heating today the Yule log has survived in many homes in England and America as an old and cherished Christmas tradition, though actually it originated among the Germanic tribes as a pagan celebration for the Yule-god Thor at the time of the solstice.

CHAPTER 12

The Christmas Tree

The Christmas tree is the main feature of modern Christmas celebrations. It is completely Christian in origin and historians have never been able to connect it in any way with ancient Germanic or Asiatic mythology. Surprising as it may seem, the use of Christmas trees is a fairly recent custom in all countries outside of Germany, and even in Germany it attained its immense popularity as recently as the beginning of the last century, although there is some evidence of its use in certain sections of Germany much earlier.

The origin of the Christmas tree goes back to the medieval German mystery plays. One of the most popular "mysteries" was the Paradise play, representing

117

the creation of man, the sin of Adam and Eve and their expulsion from Paradise. It usually closed with the consoling promise of the coming Saviour and with a reference to His incarnation. This made the Paradise play a favorite pageant for Advent, and its closing scenes used to lead directly into the story of Bethlehem.

These plays were performed either in the open, on the large squares in front of churches, or inside the house of God. The garden of Eden was indicated by a fir tree hung with apples; it represented both the "Tree of Life" and the "Tree of discernment of good and evil" which stood in the center of Paradise (Genesis 2, 9). When the pageant was performed in church, the *Paradeisbaum* (tree of Paradise) was usually surrounded by lighted candles. Inside this ring of lights the play was enacted.

After the suppression of the mystery plays in churches, the Paradise tree, the only symbolic object of the play, found its way into the homes of the faithful, especially since many plays had interpreted it as a symbol of the coming Saviour. Following this symbolism, in the fifteenth century the custom developed of decorating the Paradise tree, already bearing apples, with small white wafers representing the Holy Eucharist; thus, believed the faithful, the tree which had borne the fruit of sin for Adam and Eve, now bore the saving fruit of the Sacrament, symbolized by the wafers. These wafers were later replaced by little

118

pieces of pastry cut in the shape of stars, angels, hearts, flowers, and bells. And finally, other cookies were introduced bearing the shape of men, birds, dogs, roosters, lions, and other animals. Tradition, however, called for the latter being cut from brown dough while the first group was made of white dough.

Up to the middle of the seventeenth century the *Christbaum* (as the tree is called in German) had no lights. The Christmas candles, generally used in medieval times, were placed on the Christmas pyramid made of graduated wooden shelves. As time went on, however, the tree replaced the pyramid in its function of representing Christ as the Light of the world: the candles and glittering decorations were transferred from the pyramid to the tree; and thus the modern Christmas tree was finally evolved with its familiar features: lights, candy canes, glass balls (remember puffed wheat and cranberries strung like a necklace?), and many other colorful features. In Europe cookies, sweets, and oranges were, and still are, more often used. A star in some form usually decorates the top of the tree.

A reminder of the origin of our modern Christmas tree may still be found in sections of Bavaria where fir branches and little trees, decorated with lights, apples, and tinsel, are still called *Paradeis*.

It seems fairly certain that the original home of the Christmas tree is the left bank of the upper Rhine in

Germany where this transformation of the tree took place during the fifteenth century. The first mention of the tree as it is now known (but still without lights) dates from the Alsace (1521). A detailed description is given in a manuscript from Strasbourg (1605). At that time the tree was widely accepted in those parts. In the course of the following centuries it slowly became popular in other parts of Germany. It wasn't until the beginning of the nineteenth century, however, that it spread rapidly and grew into a widespread German custom, from whence it was taken up by the Slavic people in Eastern Europe.[36]

The Christmas tree was introduced into France in 1837, when Princess Helen of Mecklenburg brought it to Paris after her marriage to the Duke of Orleans. It was brought to England around the middle of the last century when Prince Albert of Saxony, the husband of Queen Victoria, had a tree set up at Windsor Castle in 1841. From the royal court the fashion spread, first among the nobility, then among the people in general, until by the second half of the last century it was very much a part of the English Christmas celebration.

The tree came to America as a cherished companion of the German immigrants. The first wave of German immigration, about 1700, brought thousands of Protestant farmers from the Rhine provinces (Palatinate) who, after much suffering and many adventures in the colony of New York, finally settled in western Pennsylvania. The descendants of these early immigrants still inhabit the Lebanon valley, keeping most of their ancient customs.

The second wave of German immigration began about 1830. These people, made up of both Catholic and Protestant groups, settled in New York, New England, on the farms of Ohio and Wisconsin, and other parts of America. Through them the Christmas tree was brought to the attention of their neighbors, and soon became a much admired and familiar sight in all the churches of German settlements and in the homes of German-Americans everywhere.

In spite of the official suppression of Christmas in New England, the custom of the Christmas tree spread. The fact that the royalty in England had adopted it, did much to make it fashionable in the homes of Americans of English descent. Wherever new settlements sprang up in the middle and far West, the founders always brought with them the Christmas tree custom from the East.

The tree which in 1850 had been called "a new German toy" by Charles Dickens, was termed "old-fashioned" by President Harrison in 1891 when, on December twenty-second of that year, speaking to reporters about the Christmas celebration at the White House, he said, "And we shall have an old-fashioned Christmas tree for the grandchildren upstairs." [37]

America has added one new feature to the traditional

121

use of the tree. It was here that the custom originated of setting up lighted Christmas trees in public places, just as outdoor cribs, European in character, are to be found in many large cities now at Christmas time, the most noted of all the famous one each year on Boston Common.

The originating of the Christmas tree is sometimes ascribed to Martin Luther, although we have no historical evidence of any kind for this. Luther might have used the tree, but its origin, symbolism, and name go far beyond him into earlier German history.

In America many places claim the honor of putting up the first Christmas tree. As a matter of fact, German immigrants, especially those from the upper Rhine, are most likely to have set up the first Christmas trees in America, in their own homes as early as 1710. The Christmas tree became fairly well known to the general public here about the middle of the nineteenth century through German Catholics and Lutherans. It soon caught everybody's fancy and spread like wildfire, and of course now is the most beloved popular feature of the Christmas season.

CHAPTER 13

Christmas Plants
and Flowers

The custom of decorating homes on festive days is world-wide. It is neither pagan nor Christian in itself but rather a natural expression of joy mingled with solemnity. It has been practiced in all parts of the world for thousands of years. When the early Christians, however, began to use laurel branches for festive decoration, the Church discouraged the idea because the display of laurel had been associated with the feast of the Saturnalia and other pagan festivals of the Roman Empire. The great writer, Tertullian (third century), says in his treatise on idolatry: "Let those who have no Light burn their (pagan) lamps daily. Let those who

123

face the fire of hell affix laurels to their door-posts. . . . You are a light of the world, a tree ever green; if you have renounced the pagan temple, make not your home such a temple!" [38]

When Tertullian wrote this warning, he certainly was unaware that the words he chose gave the Christians further motive for expressing in symbols his phrase: "You are a light, a tree ever green."

The Church gradually accepted and blessed the practice of decorating both the house of God and the Christian home with plants and flowers on the feast of the Lord's Nativity. Pope St. Gregory I (604) in a letter to St. Augustine of Canterbury advises him to permit, and even to encourage, harmless popular customs which in themselves are not pagan but natural, and could be given Christian interpretation. [39]

The plants used traditionally as Christmas decorations are mostly evergreens: first, because they were the only ones available in the winter season; secondly, because from ancient times the evergreens have been symbolic of *eternal life*.

In this country the use of plants and flowers to adorn churches, homes, communities, and schools during the sacred season has long been a popular custom. Fir, spruce, holly, and yew are the plants used on the continent of Europe to deck the homes at Christmas time. In England, holly, laurel, mistletoe, and rosemary are favorite Christmas decorations. In Mexico and this

124

country, the beautiful poinsettia plant is often used at Christmas.

The Mistletoe · In many American homes, especially among families originating in the British Isles, a cluster of mistletoe is hung, shimmering with silver pearls and pale green leaves, above the door, on the walls, or from the ceiling of the room.

The mistletoe was a sacred plant in the pagan religion of the Druids in Britain. It was believed to have all sorts of miraculous qualities: the power of healing diseases, making poisons harmless, giving fertility to humans and animals, protection from witchcraft, banning evil spirits, bringing good luck and great blessings. In fact, it was considered so sacred that even enemies who happened to meet beneath a mistletoe in the forest would lay down their arms, exchange a friendly greeting, and keep a truce until the following day. From this old custom grew the practice of suspending mistletoe over a doorway or in a room as a token of good will and peace to all comers. A kiss under the mistletoe was interpreted as a sincere pledge of love and a promise of marriage and, at the same time, it was an omen of happiness, good fortune, fertility, and long life to the lovers who sealed and made known their engagement by a kiss beneath the sacred plant.

How did it happen that the mistletoe became a Christmas decoration and a Christmas symbol? After

Britain was converted from paganism to Christianity, the Bishops did not allow the mistletoe to be used in churches because it had been the main symbol of a pagan religion. Even to this day mistletoe is rarely used as a decoration for altars. There was, however, one exception. At the Cathedral of York, at one period before the Reformation, a large bundle of mistletoe was brought into the sanctuary each year at Christmas and solemnly placed on the altar by a priest. In this rite the plant which the Druids had called "All-heal" was used as a symbol of Christ, the Divine Healer of nations.

The people of England then adopted the mistletoe as a decoration for their homes at Christmas. Its old, pagan religious meaning was soon forgotten but some of the other meanings and customs have survived: the kiss under the mistletoe; the token of good will and friendship; the omen of happiness and good luck; and the new religious significance:

> The mistletoe bough at our Christmas board
> Shall hang, to the honor of Christ the Lord:
> For He is the evergreen tree of Life. . . .

The Holly · This plant has always been a significant part of Christmas decorations, here and in the British Isles. When the earth turns brown and cold, the holly with its shiny green leaves and bright red berry seems to lend itself naturally to Christmas decoration, as described in this traditional English carol:

126

The holly and the ivy,
    When they are both full grown,
Of all the trees that are in the woods,
    The holly bears the crown.

To the early Christians in Northern Europe this plant was a symbol of the burning thorn bush of Moses, and the flaming love for God that filled Mary's heart. Its prickly points, and red berries resembling drops of blood, also reminded the faithful that the Divine Child was born to wear a crown of thorns.

Not only is holly hung at doors and windows, on tables and walls, but its green leaves and red berries have become the universal symbol of Christmas, adorning greeting cards, gift tags and labels, gift boxes, and wrapping paper at Christmas time.

Medieval superstition in England endowed holly with a special power against witchcraft; unmarried women were told to fasten a sprig of holly to their beds at Christmas, to guard them throughout the year from being turned into witches by the Evil One. (In Germany, branches of holly that had been used as Christmas decoration in church, were brought home and superstitiously kept as charms against lightning.) Another English superstition claimed that holly brought good luck to men, and that ivy brought it to women. The holly, therefore, is always referred to as "he" while the ivy is the distaff plant:

127

> Holly and his merry men they dance and sing,
> Ivy and her maidens weep, and hands wring.

Holly is a symbol of Christmas joy and merriment. Its appearance in the homes of old England opened the season of feasting and good cheer, often with this traditional English carol so familiar in this country:

> Deck the hall with boughs of holly,
> Tra la la, etc.;
> 'Tis the season to be jolly,
> Tra la la, etc.

In this country, the native holly has almost disappeared because of the selfishness of careless holly hunters at Christmas time. What is used here now is of the European variety with larger leaves and berries and commercially grown by farmers in this country. The holly tree comes into its full fruition after about eighteen years. Many farmers in holly-growing sections plant cuttings in the month of August after the birth of their first child, hoping that a profitable crop will be ready just in time to meet college expenses years later.

The California holly (*Toyon*) grows along the Pacific coast and has extra brilliant flaming red-colored berries which are placed in Christmas wreaths of evergreen for decorations.

The Ivy · In pagan Rome the ivy was the badge of the wine-god Bacchus and displayed as a symbol of unrestrained drinking and feasting. For this reason it was later banished from Christian homes. The old tradition in England ruled that ivy should be banned from the inside of homes and should be allowed to grow only on the outside:

> Holly standeth in the hall,
>> Fair to behold;
> Ivy stands without the door,
>> She is full sore a-cold.

Accordingly, the use of ivy as a Christmas decoration was opposed by most people in medieval England; on the continent of Europe it was hardly ever used for that purpose. But a symbolism of human weakness clinging to Divine strength was frequently ascribed to the ivy, and this prompted some poets in old England to defend ivy as a decoration at Christmas time:

> Ivy, chief of trees it is,
>> The most worthy in all the town;
> He that saith other, does amiss:
>> Worthy is she to bear the crown.

Another reason for excluding ivy was its association with death, because it was generally grown in cemeteries, as Charles Dickens observed:

> Creeping where no life is seen,
> A rare old plant is the ivy green.

However, the delicate little ground ivy, "which groweth in a sweet and shadowed place," was at all times a favorite plant of the English home; it used to be kept in pots and displayed around the house not only at Christmas but all year round as well. Many of the pioneer settlers coming to the shores of the New World brought pots of such ground ivy with them. And it is really the most popular indoor as well as outdoor plant in most parts of the country today.

The Laurel (Bay) · As an ancient symbol of triumph, the laurel is aptly used for Christmas decorations, to proclaim the victory over sin and death which Christ's birth signifies. In Friesland, Germany, an old carol was sung by the men representing the Magi on Epiphany day:

> From afar we come, and our staves
>   Are adorned with laurel;
> To seek Jesus, the King, the Saviour great,
>   And to bring Him laurel.

Bay was greatly cherished as a Christmas plant in bygone centuries. "Rosemary and baies that are most faire were stuck about the houses and the churches at Christmas time," says the poet Robert Herrick. In fact, laurel was the first plant used as Christmas decoration; the early Christians at Rome adorned their homes with it, in celebration of the Nativity of Christ.

130

The modern custom of hanging laurel wreaths on the outside of doors as a friendly greeting to our fellow-men comes from an old Roman practice. The wreath was their symbol of victory, glory, joy, and celebration. The Christmas wreath did not come to America from the continent of Europe, since it was hardly used there in past centuries (except in the form of the Advent wreath). It seems to have been introduced here by the Irish immigrants and gradually became part of the American Christmas scene.

The Rosemary · This delicate plant has been connected with Christmas since time immemorial. According to an old legend it was honored by God in reward for the humble service which it offered to Mary and her Child. On the way to Egypt, so the charming story goes, Mary washed the tiny garments of Jesus and spread them over a rosemary bush to dry in the sun. Since then the rosemary has delighted man by its delicate fragrance.

In other medieval legends this plant is pictured as a great protection and help against evil spirits, especially if it has been used in church as a decoration on Christmas day.

The Cherry · It is customary among the Czechs and Slovaks, also in the Tyrol and some other sections of Central Europe, to break a branch off a cherry tree at the beginning of Advent, place it in a pot of water in

131

the kitchen and keep it in warm air. The twig then would burst into blossom at Christmas time and made a very festive decoration. Such cherry branches, brought to flowering at Christmas, were considered omens of good luck. For instance, the girl who had tended the twig would find a good husband within the year, if she succeeded in producing the bloom exactly on Christmas eve.

The famous English "Cherry tree carol" is based on a legendary service performed by the tree in connection with the Christmas story. According to this legend, Joseph is an elderly man walking with his young bride "in a garden gay, where cherries were growing on every spray." (In the original Oriental legend these trees are date palms.) When Mary asks him for cherries, being hungry for some of the fruit, he refuses with unfriendly words because he is troubled by doubts about the angel's message. But his doubts are quickly dispelled by a small miracle:

> O! then bespoke Jesus,
>   All in his mother's womb,
> "Go to the tree, Mary,
>   And it shall bow down;
>
> "Go to the tree, Mary,
>   And it shall bow to thee,
> And the highest branch of all
>   Shall bow down to Mary's knee.

132

"And she shall gather cherries
    By one, by two, by three."
"Now you can see, Joseph,
    Those cherries were for me."

O! eat your cherries, Mary,
    O! eat your cherries now.
O! eat your cherries, Mary,
    That grow on the bough.

Whereupon Joseph asks pardon for his unbecoming suspicions, as an angel appears to him, announcing that the heavenly King will soon be born.

The Poinsettia · This native plant of Central America is now widely used in churches and homes at Christmas, because the flaming star of its red bracts resembles the star of Bethlehem. It is a very popular Christmas decoration in this country, really the favorite plant of the season. The poinsettia was named after Dr. Joel Roberts Poinsett (1851), who served as United States Ambassador to Mexico. Upon his return, in 1829, he brought this flower with him to his home in South Carolina, where it flourished.

The people of Mexico call the poinsettia the "flower of the Holy Night." A charming Mexican legend explains its origin: On a Christmas eve, long ago, a poor little boy went to church in great sadness, because he had no gift to bring to the Holy Child. He dared not

133

enter the church, and, kneeling humbly on the ground outside the house of God, prayed fervently and assured our Lord with tears, how much he desired to offer Him some lovely present—"But I am very poor and dread to approach You with empty hands." When he finally rose from his knees, he saw springing up at his feet a green plant with gorgeous blooms of dazzling red. His prayer had been answered; he broke some of the beautiful twigs from the plant and joyously entered the church to lay his gift at the feet of the Christ Child. Since then the plant has spread over the whole country; it blooms every year at Christmas time with such glorious abandon that men are filled with the true holiday spirit at the mere sight of the Christmas flower, symbolic of the Saviour's birth.

CHAPTER 14

Breads and Pastries

In pre-Christian times the winter solstice was celebrated for ten or twelve days in December (*Julmond:* the month of Yule). One of the main features of the celebration consisted in rituals expressing reverence for the gift of bread, thereby winning the favor of the field-gods for the new year of planting and reaping. Agricultural fertility cults were universal among the ancient nations of Europe. Invocations, display of wheat in the homes, baking of special kinds of bread and cakes, symbolic actions to foster the fertility of the soil, honoring the spirits of ancestors who had handed down the fields and pastures, these customs were all part of their ritual.

With the coming of Christianity many of these practices were discontinued; many others, however, were never relinquished and were more or less incorporated into the celebration of Christmas, usually assuming Christian symbolism.

This dual origin of many Christmas customs has been preserved most clearly in the agricultural nations of Eastern Europe, especially among the Ukrainians, whose country still is regarded as the "bread basket" of Europe. To a Ukrainian peasant Christmas was, and still is, what Thanksgiving day is to us, a day on which he offers thanks to God for a good harvest and invokes Divine blessing for his fields in the coming year.

On Christmas eve, the father of the Ukrainian family brings into the home a sheaf of wheat from the barn, placing it upright in a corner of the room. This sheaf is called "Forefather," symbolizing those forefathers of the nation who first tilled the land. The floor is strewn with hay and straw; there is hay even on the table, on which two loaves of fragrant white bread are placed, one on top of the other, with a Christmas candle stuck in the upper loaf. The first and most important dish of the solemn dinner on Christmas eve is *Kutya*, consisting of boiled wheat with honey and poppyseed. The head of the family, after blessing this dish, takes a spoonful of it and throws it against the ceiling—an ancient symbol of thanksgiving which has survived from the pre-Christian era.

Indeed some of the Ukrainian Christmas songs contain a Christianized version of the ancient fertility cult. In one of these canticles, God and some Saints visit a peasant village, and as they sit around the table drinking wine and honey, they notice that St. Elias is missing. St. Peter is sent to look for him; he finds Elias in the fields where he is sowing wheat.

In Poland, sheaves of wheat or grain from the harvest are placed in the four corners of the principal room on Christmas eve. Straw is spread on the floor and laid on the dining table, and a clean white cloth put over it. The table, bearing the Christmas candle and dishes with traditional pastry, is placed in front of the family shrine—usually a statue of Christ or the Blessed Virgin.

Meanwhile the children watch impatiently for the appearance of the first star in the frosty sky. Its light is the signal for the beginning of the *vigilia*, the meatless Christmas eve dinner. The Christmas candle is lit and all other lights are extinguished as the whole family kneels in prayer before the shrine. Then the Father breaks the Christmas wafers (*Oplatek*), which have been blessed by the priest, and distributes them, kissing each member of the family and wishing them a joyful feast. The dinner consists of Polish dishes (*barzch, pierogi*), various kinds of fish, nuts, plums, and Christmas pastry (*strucle, makowninki*). A lovely custom is the setting of a special place for anyone who might knock at the door that night.

137

After the meal the candles on the Christmas tree are lit and the children receive their gifts. The rest of the evening is spent in prayer and carol singing in preparation for midnight Mass.

In most countries the Christmas cakes which were baked on the eve of the feast and eaten during the season were said to bring special blessings of good luck and health. In Ireland, England, and Scotland a cake was baked on Christmas eve for every member of the household. These were usually circular in shape and flavored with caraway seeds. If anyone's cake happened to break, it was an omen of bad luck. The Irish people have a Gaelic name for Christmas eve, *Oidhche na ceapairi*, which means "Night of Cakes." [40] In Germany and France, Christmas cakes were often adorned with the figure of the Holy Child, made of sugar. The Greek Christmas cakes had a cross on top, and one such cake was left on the table during Holy Night in the hope that Christ Himself would come and eat it. The Christmas loaf (*Pain calendeau*) is still made in southern France; it is quartered crosswise and is eaten only after the first quarter has been given to some poor person. In central and eastern Germany a special bread is made of wheat flour, butter, sugar, almond, and raisins (*Christstollen*). Slavic nations (Poles, Russians, Lithuanians, Rumanians, etc.) prepare in addition to their Christmas loaves thin wafers of white flour which are eaten (often with syrup or honey) before the main

138

meal on Christmas eve. The Lithuanians call these wafers "bread of the angels." Various scenes of the Nativity are imprinted on them, and the head of the household distributes them among his family, as a symbol of love and peace. In Russia, St. Nicholas (*Kolya*) puts wheat cakes on the windowsills during Holy Night. Among the nations of Central Europe fruit bread (*Kletzenbrot*) and fruit cake are favorite Christmas dishes. In France and French Canada no one dreams of going to a store to buy bread during the Christmas season, for the mothers bake a large batch of small round loaves in honor of the Feast (*pain d'habitant*).

Even more abundant and varied are the many forms of Christmas pastries, cookies, and sweets which have survived to the present and, in some countries, as a substitute for the ancient cakes. In Germany, Austria, Switzerland, and other regions of Central Europe, the Christmas pastry (*Weihnachtsgebäck*) consists of various forms, different in shape and composition. Christmas tree pastry (*Christbaumgebäck*) is made of a white dough and cut in the shape of stars, angels, flowers, and animals. It was, and still is, hung on the tree and eaten by the children when the tree is taken down. The honey pastry (*Honigbackwerk*) is made of flour, honey, ginger and other spices and it is a favorite Christmas dish all over Germany (*Lebkuchen, Pfefferkuchen, Pfeffernüsse*). Another pastry, baked very hard, are the South German *Springerle,* cookies rec-

139

tangular in shape with pictures stamped on them such as flowers, animals, dancing figures, and many Christmas symbols.

The Scandinavians bake their Christmas pastry in the form of a boar or he-goat (*Juleber, Julgat*). It is served at Christmas with the other dishes but not eaten until January nineteenth, the feast day of St. Canute (Martyr, King of Denmark, died 1086). A familiar Spanish Christmas sweet is the *dulces de almendra,* a pastry made of sugar, flour, egg-white, and almonds. Similar almond pastries are used during this season in Portugal and Italy. Central and South American people enjoy an unusual pastry, *bunuelos* baked of white flour, very crisp and brittle, and eaten with syrup or honey. In Venezuela the *hallaca* is the national Christmas dish, a pie of chopped meat wrapped up in a crust of corn pastry. The French and French Canadians have doughnuts (*beignes*) made of a special dough, also fruit cake and white cream-fudge (*sucre à la crème*) and a cake of whole wheat, brown sugar, and dates (*carreaux aux dattes*). The Lithuanian people eat little balls of hard and dry pastry (*Kukuliai*) which are softened in plain water.

A delightful custom, still practiced in parts of England and France, is the "Kings' Cake" baked on Epiphany day, in honor of the Magi (January 6). A coin is put into the dough before baking, and the person who finds it in his piece is the "king." In French

140

Canada this cake (*gâteau des Rois*) contains a bean and a pea, making the respective finders "king" and "queen" of the feast. Robert Herrick's "Twelfe Night" refers to this old custom:

> Now, now the mirth comes
> With the cake full of plums
> Where Bean's the King of the sport here,
> Beside we must know,
> The Pea also
> Must revell, as Queen, in the Court here.

In recent years there have been many excellent foreign cookbooks published so that housewives of all nationalities can now bake and cook as their forefathers did in the old country. Many of these cakes and pastries are now an important part of Christmas in this country.

CHAPTER 15

The Christmas Dinner

Christmas was, and in many countries still is, preceded by a day of fasting and abstinence, in preparation for the Lord's Nativity. But on Christmas day, ever since the beginning of Christianity, a great feast was held. In the course of time naturally each nation developed its own treasured customs in connection with the Christmas dinner.

The traditional American Christmas meal is English in origin although the English "Christmas bird" (usually goose or capon) was supplanted by our turkey and cranberry sauce. The boisterous Christmas dinners of the English nobility and gentry in ancient times, with many guests, gluttonous eating and drinking, have never found their way into the New World and have long since disappeared in Britain.

An example of English Christmas feasting at the royal table in ancient times is described in a famous poem by Whistlecraft:

> They served up salmon, venison and wild boars,
> By hundreds, and by dozens and by scores.
> Hogsheads of honey, kilderkins of mustard,
> Muttons, and fatted beeves, and bacon swine;
> Herons and bitterns, peacocks, swan and bustard,
> Teal, mallard, pigeons, widgeons, and, in fine,
> Plum-puddings, pancakes, apple-pies and custard,
> And therewithal they drank good Gascon wine,
> With mead, and ale, and cider of our own. . . .

The reckless profusion of those feasts, however, had one redeeming feature: the poor were generously treated at Christmas, when incredible amounts of meat were distributed among them.

The typical English Christmas dinner in medieval times, in castle and manor, started with the serving of the "Boar's Head," which was brought in solemn procession by the chief cook, accompanied by waiters, pages, and minstrels, to the tune of the old carol, "The Boar's Head in Hand I Bear . . ." Then followed other courses in bewildering variety. Here is the bill-of-fare for such a dinner, held about 1560, which consisted of seventeen main dishes: roast boar with mustard; a

143

boiled capon; a boiled haunch of beef; roasted beef tongue; a roasted pig; mince pie; roast beef; a roasted goose; a roasted swan; roast turkey; venison; pasty of venison; a kid with a pudding in the belly; olive pie; a couple of roasted capons; custard. Sixteen other dishes contained salads, fricassees, pastry and sweets, not to mention the accessories like bread, herbs, carrots, parsnips, turnips, and celery. (Potatoes were not introduced until 1586 and did not come into general use until about one hundred years later.)

On Christmas, 1770, the Hon. Sir Henry Grey, Baronet, of London, ordered a pie containing two bushels of flour, twenty pounds of butter, four geese, two turkeys, two rabbits, four wild ducks, two woodcocks, six snipes, four partridges, two beef tongues, seven blackbirds, and six pigeons. The pie was nine feet in circumference, resting in a case on wheels, and had to be pushed into the dining room by two men.[41] It would be difficult to imagine which was more obnoxious, the sight of it or the taste of the mixture. Such extravagance was the fashion in Britain for centuries.

Among the common people, a large bird was the standard fare at Christmas dinners: goose, capon, bustard, or chicken; and, after 1550, turkey, which had been brought from Mexico to Europe at the beginning of the sixteenth century and was soon domesticated in Spain, France, and England.

Early Christmas dinners in this country, so modest

and simple compared to the English fare, bring home the fact that it was not the royalty and nobility, but the poor, common people who brought their English habits and customs to the colonies. The good Lord even had turkeys ready for them when they reached the shores of the New World, although the wild, North American bird was a dry, tough, and cheerless morsel in the early days. But the Americans stood by it, righteously refusing to return to the flesh-pots of old British Christmas dinners, even when they later could afford it. Instead, they developed and improved the strain of the native bird until it became the meaty delicacy of today, the golden center of our Christmas meal.

Christmas, the feast of good cheer, has always been a favorite occasion for drinking, especially so in recent times, where hard liquor often replaces the sweet ciders and light wines of more temperate days. The Latin nations enjoyed, and still do, their customary wine with the Christmas meal. In northern Europe, beer was a favorite drink; in England, ale.

A Christmas drink peculiar to the English was the "wassail," always served in a large bowl. The word comes from the old Saxon and used to be a drinker's greeting (*Was haile:* your health). It usually consisted of ale, roasted apples, eggs, sugar, nutmeg, cloves, and ginger, drunk while hot. From this custom of drinking the wassail, the English derived the word "wassailing"

145

for any kind of Christmas revels which were accompanied by drinking.

It was not until the eighteenth century that the mild wassail drink was gradually supplanted by a punch made up of stronger spirits. The punch bowl finally replaced the wassail bowl and is now a popular feature of Christmas in this country.

In a lovely old European custom on December twenty-seventh, St. John's Day, the Church bestows a special blessing on wine. This is an old rite in honor of St. John the Evangelist who, according to legend, drank a glass of poisoned wine without suffering harm. Anyone may have wine blessed by a priest on St. John's Day with a special blessing.[42] In times past, and even today in some countries, this wine is taken with the mutual wish: "Drink the love of St. John!" meaning the love of God and men of which St. John is such an eloquent herald in his sacred writings.

CHAPTER 16

The Battle of the Mince Pie

Mince pie on the Christmas table is an old English custom. When the Puritans in New England tried to supplant Christmas with Thanksgiving (and almost succeeded for a time), they also transferred the English Christmas dinner of "a bird" and mince pie to their new feast day. Thus the good Puritans, very much against their intentions, have provided us, by a turn of events, with a second Christmas dinner each year (Thanksgiving and Christmas).

The British had various kinds of "minc'd pie" long before it became a part of the Christmas meal. The Christmas pie was born when the Crusaders, returning

147

from the Holy Land, brought along all sorts of Oriental spices. So, it followed that the Lord's Nativity had to be celebrated with a pie containing the spices from His native land.

What concoctions the mince pies were in those early days! A recipe for a Christmas pie, made in 1394, mentions the following ingredients: a pheasant, a hare, a capon, two partridges, two pigeons, and two rabbits; their meat separated from the bones, to be chopped into a fine hash; add the livers and hearts of all these animals, also two kidneys of sheep; add little meat balls of beef, with eggs; add pickled mushrooms, salt, pepper, vinegar, and various spices, pour into it the broth in which the bones were cooked. Put all into a crust of good pastry and bake. . . . Wonder indeed, that, according to an old English saying, "the devil dares not show himself in Cornwall at Christmas time lest he should be baked in a pie." [43]

A Christmas mince pie of the seventeenth century, according to Robert Herrick, was filled with beef tongues, chopped chicken, eggs, raisins, orange and lemon peelings, sugar, and various spices. In this recipe it is not difficult to recognize the basic pattern of modern mince pie.

Another national Christmas dish in England was (and still is with variations) the famous plum pudding. It was bound up in a cloth, boiled on Christmas morning, and served with great ceremony, often saturated with alcohol and set aflame while being borne into the dining room, as Dickens describes so vividly in his *Christmas Carol*. The name dates from the end of the seventeenth century. Before that time it was called "hackin" because its ingredients were hacked or chopped before being mixed into the pie.

Of historical interest is the fact that in England, before the Reformation, a peculiar Christmas custom had grown and rapidly spread through the country. In honor of the Saviour's humble birth, the mince pies were made in oblong form, representing the manger; and sometimes, in the slight depression on top of the pie was placed a little figure of the child Jesus. Thus the pie was served, as an object of devotion as well as part of the feast. The "baby" was removed and the "manger" was eaten with great glee by the children.

After the Reformation, the Puritans started a great and vehement outcry against the mince pie. It was not the pie itself which aroused their wrath, but its form, and the figure of the child. However, in their fervor they did not distinguish the issues and directed their attack against the dish itself. The "battle of the mince pie" was on and raged for many years.[44]

The Puritans were convinced that to eat mince pie at Christmas was an abomination, idolatry, superstition, and a popish observance. The Catholics and Anglicans immediately rose to the defense of the cherished dish. The more the Puritans condemned it, the more

149

did the others make and eat it. The eating or non-eating of mince pie thus became a test of orthodoxy on either side.

When the Puritans finally came to power, mince pie, like Christmas itself, was forbidden. John Taylor (an English poet) wrote somewhat cynically, in 1646, that among other things, the eating of a Christmas pie was enough to have a man arrested for committing "high Parliament treason." [45] It was not difficult to foresee which side would be victorious in the battle. Despite the threats and solemn prohibitions, the eating of the pie was continued throughout the country. With the downfall of the Puritan regime and the restoration of the monarchy in 1660, the old mince pie returned once more to the English home, openly and legally, as a feature of the Christmas celebration.

But, ironically enough, the Puritans also won their victory. For the Catholics and Anglicans, while campaigning for the very existence of the pie and winning the struggle, had gradually neglected its shape. By the end of the seventeenth century the pie was made in circular form; the figure of the child had disappeared, and, after the smoke of the battle cleared away, both parties felt contented with their respective victories: the Catholics and Anglicans rejoiced in having saved the pie, the Puritans in having changed its form.

Thus the mince pie was brought to this country in its new circular shape. From New England it spread all over the United States and now among all our national groups is the featured dessert on Christmas day. The old quarrels have been forgotten, and Americans of every denomination eat their mince pie without qualms of conscience, in contentment and good will.

CHAPTER 17

Saint Nicholas

One of the most beloved of all the Saints long ago was St. Nicholas of Myra. In many parts of Europe children still believe St. Nicholas appears to them on the eve of his Feast (December sixth) laden with gifts. His role is that of a heavenly messenger, coming at the beginning of Advent and admonishing little children to prepare their hearts for properly welcoming the Christ Child at Christmas. He is usually impersonated by a man wearing a long white beard, dressed in the vestments of a bishop, with miter and crozier, a friendly and saintly figure, who comes down from heaven once a year to visit the children, whose patron saint he is. He examines them, questioning them on their Catechism and hearing their prayers. After entreating them to be good boys and girls and to get ready for a devout and holy Christmas, he distributes candy and fruit and departs with a loving farewell, leaving the little ones filled with holy awe and joy.

Despite the immense popularity of St. Nicholas during the Middle Ages, both in Europe and Christian Asia, there is scarcely any definite historical fact known about him except that he was Bishop of Myra in Asia Minor; that he was cast into exile and prison during the persecution of Emperor Diocletian and released by Constantine the Great; that he died in Myra about 350 and in the year 1087 his body was brought by Italian merchants from Myra to the city of Bari in Italy, where his relics are still preserved and venerated in the church of San Nicola. The reports of numerous miracles ascribed to the Saint, both before and after his death, are based on a long tradition. As early as 450, churches were being built in his honor, and his veneration was general in the Greek Church. From there, at the end of the tenth century, it spread to the German Empire, and reached its height when his relics arrived in Italy during the eleventh century. The Church celebrates his feast day as a bishop and confessor annually on December sixth.

By the year 1200, this much loved Saint had captured the hearts and imaginations of all European nations. Many churches, towns, provinces, and countries venerated him as their patron saint. He is patron of Greece, Russia, Sicily, and Lorraine; of many cities in Germany, Austria, Switzerland, Holland, and Italy. Merchants, bakers, and mariners among others have made him their patron. But he was always best known as the patron saint of children.

The beautiful legend of St. Nicholas might be told to children something like this:

St. Nicholas was born of a rich and noble family in the city of Parara in Asia Minor. When he was very little he lost his mother and father and had to live the sad and lonely life of an orphan. After he had grown to young manhood, he decided to devote his life entirely to the service of God, doing good works for his fellow-men. Obeying the words of Christ, he distributed all his possessions to the poor, the sick, and the suffering. He is said to have secretly helped very poor people by putting gifts of money through their windows during the night, when no one could see him (just as he now brings his gifts to you during the night).

His love for the Christ Child inspired him to make a pilgrimage to the Holy Land and offer prayers in those historical and holy places. On this trip a terrible storm arose but, by his prayers, he miraculously saved the already sinking ship as it tossed and turned in the high seas. That is the reason he is now venerated as a patron of mariners by many brave sailors all over the world.

When he returned home from this pilgrimage, the bishops of Asia Minor elected him as successor to the Bishop of Myra, who had just died. The whole city rejoiced when they heard of his appointment. Nicholas received the holy orders, modestly and devoutly, and as Bishop, practiced not only great holiness of life, by fasting and prayer, but had boundless love for his fellow-men. Having been an orphan himself, he now became the beloved father of widows and orphans. His constant kindness and charity were bestowed especially on the children, whom he often gathered about him, instructing them in the word of God and delighting them with many little gifts.

Under the Roman Emperor Diocletian, who persecuted the Christians, St. Nicholas was taken from his home, exiled and imprisoned. He suffered hardships of hunger, thirst, cold, loneliness, and chains. He wanted to die as a martyr. But when Emperor Diocletian left his throne and the first Christian Emperor, Constantine the Great, ruled the Roman lands, all Christians who had suffered in prison because of their faith, were released. Among them was St. Nicholas, who was able to return to Myra where he lived for many years, a kind father to all his flock especially the poor.

One day he became very ill and soon he realized it was time for him to go to Heaven. There he was met by many angels who conducted his soul to the throne of God. St. Nicholas was very happy.

155

The whole city mourned his passing, most of all little children. But very soon they found out that even from Heaven he continued to help them, if only they asked him. So the children started praying to St. Nicholas and the faithful believed their prayers were answered by thousands of miracles, small ones and great ones. To this day boys and girls all over the world pray to their patron saint, St. Nicholas.

CHAPTER 18

The Significance of Exchanging Presents

Christmas is the season for exchanging presents. It is not difficult to understand why people should be filled with good will on the Christ Child's birthday. "As long as you did it for one of these, the least of my brethren, you did it for me" (Matthew 25, 40).

The practice of present-giving was also an old Roman custom called *Strenae*. On New Year's day the people of ancient Rome exchanged gifts of sweet pastry, lamps, precious stones, and coins of gold or silver as tokens of their good wishes for a happy year. This custom, and even its name (*étrennes*), has been preserved among the French people to the present day. In most

157

countries, however, the present-giving has become a part of the actual Christmas celebration.

In Germany the packages of Christmas gifts were called by the inspired name of "Christ-bundles." It is interesting to read in books of the seventeenth century what these bundles contained. One list enumerates the following things: candy, sugar plums, cakes, apples, nuts, dolls, and toys; useful things like clothes, caps, mittens, stockings, shoes, and slippers; and things "that belong to teaching, obedience and discipline," as ABC tables, paper, pencils, books; and the "Christ-rod." This rod, attached to the bundle, was a pointed reminder for good behavior.

Another form of presenting gifts was the old German custom of the "Christmas ship" in which bundles for the children were stored away. This was adopted in England to some extent, but never attained general popularity, though special carols for the occasion were sung in both countries.

> There gently sails a precious boat,
>   It comes with rich and sacred load:
> It bears the son of God benign,
>   The loving Father's Word Divine.

And an English carol of the sixteenth century on the same theme:

> There came a ship far sailing then,
>   Saint Michael was the steersman,

Saint John sat in the horn.
Our Lord harped, our Lady sang,
And all the bells of heaven rang
On Christmas in the morn.

A popular Christmas custom in Britain is "boxing" on the feast of St. Stephen, December twenty-sixth. It originated because in medieval times the priests would empty the alms-boxes in all churches on the day after Christmas and distribute the gifts to the poor of the parish. In imitation of this church practice, the workers, apprentices, and servants kept their own personal "boxes" made of earthenware in which they stored savings and donations throughout the year. At Christmas came the last and greatest flow of coins, collected from patrons, customers, and friends. Then, on the day after Christmas, the box was broken and the money counted. This custom was eventually called "boxing" (giving and accepting presents). Each present is a "box," and the day of present-giving is "boxing-day."

A similar custom prevailed in Holland and some parts of Germany, where children were taught to save their pennies in a pig-shaped earthenware box. This box was not to be opened until Christmas and consequently was called the "feast pig." (From this custom, we now have our "piggy banks.")

Exchanging Christmas presents in this country is a combination of two old European customs. The first

159

was the present-giving of St. Nicholas, who deposited his gifts (of minor size and value) in stockings suspended for that purpose by the children on the eve of his feast day, December sixth. The second custom was that of the actual Christmas presents which the children believed the child Jesus brought on December twenty-fifth, or Christmas eve, which were arranged beneath the Christmas tree. Our present-day celebration of Christmas is a happy combination of both customs.

Who was supposed to bring the Christmas gifts to the children in the course of centuries? In most European countries the child Jesus is the gift-bringer. The children believe he comes with angels during the night, trimming the tree and putting the presents under it. Sometimes the Divine Child was impersonated by a girl dressed in white, but this custom was never widespread. The general practice had the Christ Child arrive unseen by the children; helped by the parents, like the American version of Santa Claus, He prepared the tree and distributed the gifts. When everything was ready, a little bell was rung and the anxious children entered the room where all the presents were spread out before their shining eyes. But the child Jesus, with His angels, had already left for some other home. The reading of the Christmas Gospel, a prayer before the crib, and the singing of a hymn united the whole family in the Christmas spirit before the gifts were opened.

160

This custom still survives in some parts of Germany, Austria, and other countries of Central Europe, as well as in France, French Canada, Spain, Central and South America. In Spain and Spanish-speaking countries the child Jesus (*el Niño Jesus*) brings the Christmas gifts for the children during Holy Night. Since the crib has been set up for nine days with an empty manger, the children are familiar with it. On Christmas morning, however, they find the Holy Child in the crib and the gifts arranged in front of it. They exclaim how good the *niño Jesus* was to bring them when He came down from Heaven to take up His abode in the manger in their very own home.

The German name of the Christ Child is *Christkind*, commonly used in its diminutive form *Christkindel* (both i's are short). When German immigration to New York and other eastern cities of the United States increased after the middle of the last century, the *Christkindel* of the immigrants was gradually adopted in the form of Kris Kringle, or Santa Claus, by their fellow countrymen.

In Rome and other cities of Italy an unusual figure impersonates the gift-bringer for children. It is the "Lady Befana" (or, Bufana), a sort of fairy queen. She has no relation to Christmas, however, for the day she distributes presents is January sixth (Epiphany), when the children roam the streets, happily blow their paper trumpets, and receive the gifts which Lady Befana has

161

provided for them. The name comes from the word "Epiphany."

The gift-bringer in Russia is a legendary old woman called *Babushka* (Grandmother). She is said to have misdirected the Magi when they inquired their way to Bethlehem. According to another version she refused hospitality to the Holy Family on its way to Egypt. Whatever her fault, she repented of her unkindness, and to make reparation for her sin she now goes about the world on Christmas eve, looking for the Christ Child and distributing gifts to the children. Another Russian legendary figure is Kolya (Nicholas), who goes about during Holy Night, putting on windowsills little wheat cakes which have to be eaten on Christmas day. To him is addressed a popular Russian carol:

> Kolya, Kolya,
> On Christmas eve, when all is still,
> He puts his cakes on the windowsill.
>
> Kolya, Kolya,
> Come this Holy Night, we pray,
> Come and bring us Christmas day!

CHAPTER 19

Santa Claus

After the Reformation, the feast and veneration of St. Nicholas were abolished in many countries, and the new figure of the Christmas Man substituted, so that soon the people in those countries forgot St. Nicholas who had once been so dear to them. Only here and there a trace of the traditional Christmas Saint would linger on, as, for example, the pageant of the "boy bishop" in England; or in the name *Pelznickel* (fur-Nicholas) which many people in western Germany gave to their Christmas Man (*Pels-nichol* now among the Pennsylvania Dutch).

In Holland, however, it was not so easy to obliterate the memory of the Saint because the Hollanders, a

163

nation of seafarers, had also venerated him for centuries as the patron of their ships. Dutch boats used to carry a statue of the Saint as the figure-head on their prows. When the Calvinists in Holland undertook to replace St. Nicholas with the Nordic figure of the Christmas Man, they did not succeed beyond obliterating the details of his religious past. To this day the hero of Dutch Christmas lore stubbornly retains his popular name of *Sinter Klaas*, as well as his Bishop's garments. The belief that he visited little children on the eve of his feast day was never abandoned, and his annual arrival in Holland has remained the same over the years. He comes mounted on a white charger, in awe-inspiring majesty, visiting the homes much like Santa Claus, except that there is more religious significance.

Wherever the Hollanders settled in the New World, whether in the first Dutch colony of New Amsterdam on Manhattan Island, or later in the colonies along the shores of the Hudson, they celebrated their feasts in the traditional way. The gift-bringer was good old St. Nicholas, the Bishop, who came on the eve of December sixth to fill their children's wooden clogs with his presents.

After Britain established the colony of New York, the English settlers and immigrants found the kindly figure of *Sinter Klaas*, in his becoming robes, more appealing than their own "Father Christmas," especially since St. Nicholas was so closely associated with gift-bearing to

164

children, a custom which was not practiced by Father Christmas in England.

During the eighteenth century St. Nicholas gradually became the accepted gift-bringer for most children in New York, and, adhering to the Dutch pronunciation, the word "Santa Claus" was coined from their *Sinter Klaas*. The venerable figure was then tossed into the melting pot of Americanization. Santa Claus no longer appeared as a Bishop, but as a combination of Father Christmas and St. Nicholas, and his visit was transferred from the eve of December sixth to Christmas. In place of the Bishop's robes he donned the secular dress of Father Christmas, but kept the cheerful colors of his past, the popular Dutch form of his name, and also St. Nicholas' legendary practice of depositing his gifts during the night in shoes or stockings. From the "Christmas Man" he acquired his home and work factory at the North Pole, the sleigh and the reindeer and the custom of sliding down the chimney, so familiar to all in Moore's popular poem, "'Twas the Night Before Christmas."

During the nineteenth century the figure of Santa Claus became a household word in New England, in fact along the whole eastern seaboard. From there it spread rapidly through the rest of the country, and now millions of children thrill in delight and awe at the sight of him. They tell him what they want for Christmas; they write letters to him; they give him the complete affection and confidence of their hearts—unaware of his "split" personality.

The modern story of Santa Claus, as told now to children, is more of a fairy tale. Its historical background and the charming legend of St. Nicholas are not generally known. There have been many changes made since the days of gentle St. Nicholas, whose impersonation once appeared to children, they believed, as a messenger of the Christ Child.

It has been suggested by many who have the welfare of children at heart that Santa be restored to his original Christian meaning. That would not mean changing the modern story but simply adding historical facts and some legends concerning beloved St. Nicholas to present-day Santa Claus lore. It is believed that if, at the very beginning, children could be told the historical facts about Santa Claus and his life, and the spiritual meaning of the legend, it will never cause them to be disillusioned or utter the erroneous statement, "There is no Santa Claus." The rest of the story, containing the fairy tale, will then be regarded as a rather charming addition to the legend of St. Nicholas.

CHAPTER 20

Cherished Customs— Old and New

Advent · Soon after Christmas had been established as the special feast of the Lord's Nativity, a time for prayer and fasting was introduced in preparation for the great holiday. This sacred season, called Advent, became universal in the ninth century and is still observed very widely. It begins on the Sunday nearest the feast of St. Andrew (November thirtieth) and embraces four Sundays. The prayers and liturgical services of Advent stress the preparation for the coming of Christ and the joyful expectation of the Lord's Nativity, and, in harmony with the spirit of the sea-

167

son, very beautiful Advent customs are practiced.

A very old one, for instance, is the burning of candles every night during Advent for a few minutes, while members of the family say a common prayer in preparation for Christmas. All other lights are extinguished and only the flames of the candles spread their peaceful glow to remind the faithful that they are to prepare themselves for the advent of Christ, the Light of the World. The candles, four in number, are attached to a wreath of laurel or spruce—one candle for each week of Advent. On Christmas eve, a large candle is placed in the center of the wreath, symbolizing Christ the Lord; this is the "Christmas candle." The Advent wreath was widely used in churches and homes during past centuries, and is still used in Germany and Austria.

Another Advent custom is the practice of letter-writing by the children, the letters, of course, containing lists of what they'd like for Christmas. When they go to bed before the visit of St. Nicholas on the night of December fifth, notably in Bavaria and Austria, the children put upon the windowsills little notes which they have written or dictated, addressed to the "dear Child Jesus in Heaven." St. Nicholas is supposed to take them with him on his visit during the night. And so, when the Christ Child comes on Christmas eve, He is sure to bring at least a part of what the children asked for.

In South America the children write their notes to the "little Jesus" during the time of the *Posada* (December sixteenth to twenty-fourth) and put them in front of the crib, from whence they believe angels take them to Heaven during the night.

Up until fairly recent times, a beautiful Advent custom was practiced by shepherds in Italy. They came into the towns and cities before Christmas to greet the Madonna with the music of their simple instruments. Toward the end of last century a Roman resident described it in this way: "Since the start of Advent, from four o'clock in the morning the inhabitants of the different quarters of the city are awakened by the sweet and melancholic music of the *'pifferari'* (pipers). These are the shepherds of Sabinum and of the Abruzzi who descend annually in Advent from their mountains and stand before the images of the Madonna, placed in the streets or in shops of Rome, to announce by the sound of their reed pipes and oboes the approaching birth of the Saviour. Nothing seems more touching to me than this pious custom. The Romans, whose homes are close by these madonnas, call the pipers for the novenas; and for nine days they come assiduously to play their *Canzonetta* to the Mother of God. With their mountain caps, their green cloaks, their short sheepskin or gratchin trousers, their long hair falling on their shoulders, their handsome beards, their sparkling eyes, these

169

mountaineers present the most poetic and picturesque sight that I have ever seen." [46]

In Central and South America, the nine days before Christmas are devoted to a popular novena in honor of the Holy Child (*la novena del Niño*). In the decorated church, the crib is ready, set up for Christmas; the only figure missing is that of the Child, since the manger is always kept empty until Holy Night. The novena service consists of prayers and carol-singing accompanied by popular instruments of the castanet type. In Mexico this novena is usually held in the manner of a *Posada*. After the novena service, the children roam through the streets of the cities and towns, throwing firecrackers and rockets (much like our Fourth of July as far as the noise goes), expressing their delight over the approach of Christmas.

Still another custom, this one originating in France but spreading to many other countries, was the touching practice of having children prepare a soft bedding in the manger by using little wisps of straw as tokens of prayers and good works. Every night the child was allowed to put in the crib one token for each act of devotion or virtue performed. Thus the Christ Child, coming on Christmas day, would find an ample supply of tender straw to keep Him warm and to soften the hardness of the manger's boards.

A variation of this custom is the old Slavic tradition of having the small children sleep, not in their beds

170

during Holy Night, but on a bedding of straw and hay, to allow them to take part in the grace and privilege of the Lord's poor and humble birth. Great blessings are believed to come to the little children who are thus bedded at Christmas. The Poles, Ukrainians, and other Slavic people also put straw upon the floor, beneath the Christmas table, as a reminder that all the joys and pleasures of Christmas originate from the Holy Child who Himself was reclining in poverty and want in the stable on a bed of straw.

Greeting Cards · In the middle of the nineteenth century when postal rates became cheaper, people began to send written greetings and good wishes to their relatives and friends before the feast of Christmas. It is claimed that the first Christmas greeting card was engraved in 1842, by a 16-year-old London artist, William Maw Egley, but that it failed to arouse interest among his friends. A few years later, special cards were privately printed in Britain by a few individuals who designed them for their personal use. Sir Henry Cole in 1846 commissioned J. C. Horsley to make a card for him, "the usual size of a lady's visiting card." It was many years before the manufacture and sale of cards was commercialized. By 1860 they were on the market and were quite common by about 1868.

In America, the printing of Christmas cards was introduced by the Boston lithographer, Louis Prang,

171

a native of Breslau, Germany. Prang offered them to the public for sale in 1875. Since the present popular designs of Christmas symbols were not yet known here, he adorned his cards with Killarney roses, daisies, geraniums, apple blossoms, and similar floral motives. These first American Christmas cards, like all other products of Prang's lithographic art, are still famous among collectors because of their exquisite design and craftsmanship. A few years later he broadened his designs to include: children playing in the snow; fir trees; fireplaces; and finally Santa, himself. In 1890, when a flood of cheap and gaudy novelties in Christmas cards swamped the market (dried flowers, chenille, bits of colored glass, corks, and seaweed), Prang abruptly stopped the production of his beautiful cards to register his disgust and disappointment.

Within the last few decades the sending of Christmas cards has become more a burden of social amenity than a token of good will and brotherly affection. At present, almost two billion greeting cards are mailed annually at Christmas in this country (an average of fifty cards per family). Though many of the modern cards do not have appropriate Christmas designs, there is a tendency of late to return to the genuine spiritual tone of the season.

Of late years, though, a custom has developed (and hardly discouraged by the stores) to start celebrating Christmas almost as soon as Thanksgiving dinner is over. Small wonder a 13-year-old boy was heard to remark: "By the time Christmas comes, I'm sick and tired of it."

The Blessing of Homes · It is an ancient custom in many countries to have a priest come on the feast of Epiphany to bless the home. Here is the English translation of one of the beautiful prayers:

"Bless, O Lord, almighty God, this house, that therein be found good health, chastity, the power of spiritual victory, humility, goodness and meekness, the plenitude of the Law, and thanksgiving to God, the Father, Son and Holy Spirit: and may this blessing remain on the house and on its inhabitants. Through Christ our Lord. Amen." [47]

After the blessing the initials of the legendary names of the three Magi—Gaspar, Melchior, Baltasar—are written with white chalk on the inside of the door, framed by the number of the year, all symbols connected by signs of the cross: 19 ✝ G ✝ M ✝ B ✝ 52. [48]

The End of the Season · The end of the Christmas season varies at different places. Following the feast of the Epiphany, January sixth, twelve days after Christmas, the symbols and decorations are taken down in most countries. The liturgical season extends until January fourteenth, the Octave of Epiphany. In some places cribs and decorations are kept until Candlemas

173

day, February second. Robert Herrick, in the middle of the seventeenth century, gave the following instructions for Candlemas day:

> Down with the Rosemary, and so
>   Down with the Baies and mistletoe;
> Down with the Holly, Ivie, all
>   Wherewith ye drest the Christmas Hall.

In tracing these many and varied Christmas customs back to their original source, however, it should now be evident that they are all based on the fact that Christmas is the celebration of our Lord's Nativity. Even the remnants of ancient pagan feasts and customs which survived have been transformed into a completely Christian symbolism, all of it now an integral part of this great feast which is celebrated in countries all over the world today. The origin, meaning, and purpose of all our Christmas customs is contained in the one short phrase addressed to the Holy Child from Blessed Henry Suso's carol (1366), *In dulci Jubilo* (In Sweetest Jubilation):

> *Alpha es et O*
> Thou Art the Beginning and the End.

Reference Notes

1. *Sancti Justini Dialogus cum Tryphone Judaeo* (St. Justin, Dialogue with Trypho the Jew), chap. 78. J. P. Migne, *Patrologia Graeca*, vol. VI, col. 658. Written between A.D. 155 and 160.

2. *Sancti Hieronymi Epistola LVIII ad Paulinum* (St. Jerome, Letter 58, to Paulinus). J. P. Migne, *Patrologia Latina*, vol. XXIII, col. 581.

3. Origenes, *Contra Celsum Liber Primus* (The first book against Celsus), chap. 51. J. P. Migne, *Patrologia Graeca*, vol. XI, col. 755.

4. *Synodal Letter*, Council of Jerusalem, A.D. 836.

5. See the picture of such a crib opposite page 125 in F. W. Willam's *Mary the Mother of Jesus*, St. Louis, 1947.

6. C. C. Edgar, in *Annales du Service des Antiquites de l'Egypte*, vol. 22 (1922), p. 7 ff.

7. *Revised Standard Version of the New Testament*, New York, 1946. The explanatory addition (God) is not contained in the text of the Standard Version but was inserted by the author of this book.

8. *Sanctus Beda Venerabilis De Collectaneis* (Collected Notes). J. P. Migne, *Patrologia Latina*, vol. XCIV, col. 541.

9. *Divine Office*, Proprium of the Archdiocese of Cologne, Feast of the Translation of the Magi (July 23rd), second Nocturn.

10. Flavius Josephus, *The Jewish Antiquities*, book XV, chap. 10, par. 4.

11. *Sancti Cypriani De Pascha Computus* (The Computation of Easter). J. P. Migne, *Patrologia Latina*, vol. IV, col. 963.

12. St. John Chrysostom, *On the Solstice and Equinox*, quoted in the *Catholic Encyclopedia*, vol. III, p. 727.

13. This report was found, in direct quotation, in three books

of the last century. Inquiries at various libraries in the United States and in Canada failed to produce further data on Harrison's book.

14. *Sancti Gregorii Turonensis Libri Miraculorum,* I, 1. J. P. Migne, *Patrologia Latina,* vol. LXXI, col. 707.

15. See also R. J. Campbell, *The Story of Christmas,* New York, 1934, p. 40, where a similar legend is mentioned.

16. Thomas de Celano, *Sancti Francisci Assisiensis Vita and Miracula* (Life and Miracles of St. Francis of Assisi), critical edition, revised by P. Edward d'Alencon, Rome, 1906, chap. cli, par. 199. Quotations from this (Latin) edition were translated by the author.

17. *Hamlet,* act I, scene 1.

18. *The Flying Eagle Gazette,* London, 25 December 1652.

19. N. Doran, "The Ups and Downs of Christmas," *The National Magazine,* London, 1857.

20. "The Declaration of many thousands of the city of Canterbury . . ." (Broadsheet), London, 1648 (British Museum).

21. See W. P. Dawson, *Christmas; its Origins and Associations,* London, 1902, p. 211 ff.

22. From "Old Christmas Returned," a poem of about 1665.

23. Ildefonso Schuster, *The Sacramentary* (*Liber Sacramentorum*), New York, 1924, vol. I, p. 362.

24. Celano, *Life and Miracles of St. Francis,* chap. xxx, par. 86.

25. This poem is a part of the famous Cherry Tree Carol, rendered in the version of William Hone, *Ancient Mysteries,* London, 1823, p. 90.

26. The Latin text and the music of this carol are reprinted in *A Christmas Book,* by D. B. Wyndham Lewis and G. C. Heseltine, London, 1928, p. 77; also in *The Trapp Family Book of Christmas Songs,* edited by Franz Wasner, New York, 1950, p. 16.

27. See *The Trapp Family Singers,* Souvenir Book Publishing Co., New York, 1948, p. 4; also the article on the Rainer

Singers by Hans Nathan, in the *Musical Quarterly*, G. Schirmer, New York, January, 1946.

28. The author translated this carol from the Spanish version as published in *Edasi* magazine, Caracas (Venezuela), 1949, with permission of the publishers.

29. *The Jesuit Relations and Allied Documents*, ed. by R. G. Thwaites, Cleveland, 1896-1901. Vol. XXVII (1898), p. 210.

30. Karl Young, *The Drama of the Medieval Church*, Oxford, 1933, vol. II, p. 4 ff.

31. See Bernhard Duhr, S.J., *Geschichte der Jesuiten in den Ländern deutscher Zunge*, 6 vols., Freiburg and Regensburg, 1907-1928.

32. Notes of the pastor (Fr. Gustave Eck, S.J.), 1851, manuscript, parish archive, Holy Trinity Church, Boston, Massachusetts.

33. See Young, *The Drama of the Medieval Church*, vol. II, p. 29 ff; and William Sandys, *Christmastide*, London, s. a., p. 168. Also James L. Monks, S.J., *Great Catholic Festivals*, New York, 1951, p. 21 ff.

34. *Jesuit Relations*, vol. LXI (1900), p. 118 ff.

35. Celano, *Life and Miracles of St. Francis*, chap. xxx, par. 84-86.

36. For the historical research on the Christmas tree and other German Christmas customs, see Paul Cassel, *Weihnachten; Ursprünge, Bräuche und Aberglauben*, Berlin, 1861; A. Tille, *Geschichte der Deutschen Weihnacht*, 1893; O. Lauffer, *Der Weihnachtsbaum in Glauben und Brauch*, 1934; C. Schneider, *Der Weihnachtsbaum und seine Heimat, das Elsass*, 1929.

37. Quoted in Dawson, *Christmas, its Origins and Associations*, p. 313.

38. *Tertulliani Liber de Idololatria* (Book on Idolatry), chap. xv. J. P. Migne, *Patrologia Latina*, vol. I, col. 684.

39. St. Gregory addressed this instruction to the French abbot Mellitus, requesting him to forward it to St. Augustine of Canterbury: *Sancti Gregorii Magni Epistola LXXVI ad Mellitum Abbatem* (Letter 76, to the Abbot Mellitus). J. P. Migne, *Patrologia Latina*, vol. LXXVII, col. 1215.

40. Also *"oidhche nam bannag"*; see Edward Dwelly (comp.), *The Illustrated Gaelic Dictionary*, Fleet, Hants, 1930, p. 66.

41. From the *Newcastle Chronicle*, 6 January 1770, quoted in William Hone's *Table Book*, vol. II, p. 506.

42. *Rituale Romanum, Benedictio vini in Festo* S. *Joannis Apostoli et Evangelistae* (The Roman Ritual, Blessing of wine on the feast of St. John, Apostle and Evangelist).

43. Quoted in Crippen, *Christmas and Christmas Lore*, p. 123.

44. See Thomas K. Hervey, *The Book of Christmas*, Boston, 1888, p. 159.

45. John Taylor, *The Complaint of Christmas written after Twelftide and printed before Candlemas*, London, 1646.

46. *Dix ans au service du Roi Pie IX*. Memoires d'un zouave pontifical, par Comte Philippe de V***, Fribourg, 1880, 2 vols. Translation by Allen J. Doherty.

47. *Rituale Romanum, Benedictio domorum in Festo Epiphaniae* (Blessing of homes on the feast of the Epiphany).

48. *Rituale Romanum, Benedictio cretae in Festo Epiphaniae* (Blessing of chalk on the feast of the Epiphany).

Abruzzi, 169
Adalbert, St., 36
Adam, 118
Adam, Adolphe Charles, 87
Adeste Fideles, 87
Advent, 35, 107, 118, 131, 152, 167 ff
Afghanistan, 25
Agde, council of, 35
Albert of Saxony, Prince, 120
Alexander, 27
Alexandra, 27
Algonquins, 102
Alps, 114
Alsace, 120
America, 48, 53, 81, 86, 89, 92, 97, 102, 104, 110, 118, 116, 120, 122, 131, 142, 171
Anastasia, church of St., 35
Ancient Mysteries, 80 q.*
Andrew, St., feast of, 167
Angels, song of the, 22 f.
"Angels we have heard on high," 86
Anglican Church, 44
Anglicans, 149, 150
Ansgar, St., 36
Antipater, 27
Aphrodite, 19
Apostles, 17
Ara Coeli, church of, 109, 110

* q.—quoted

Arabia, 25
Aristobulus, 27
Arnsdorf, 89
Asia, Christian, 153
Asia Minor, 153, 154, 155
Augustine, St., 34
Augustine, St., of Canterbury, 36, 124
Austria, 49, 53, 66, 70, 75, 76, 88, 89, 97, 107, 115, 139, 154, 161, 168; Western, 36
"Away in a manger," 81

Babe, Divine, 68
Babushka, 162
Bacchus, 128
Bach, *Christmas Oratorio,* 81
Baltasar, 26, 173
Barbarossa, Emperor, 26
Bari, Italy, 153
Barnes, Edward Shippen, 86
Baroccio, *Nativity,* 23
Bavaria, 49, 53, 75, 76, 88, 115, 119, 168
Bay, *see* Laurel
Beacon Hill, 92
Bede the Venerable, St., *Collectanea et Flores,* 26 q.
Befana, Lady, 161
Bethlehem, 18, 20, 24, 26, 27, 39, 53, 74, 95, 98, 106, 107, 118, 162; massacre of, 26 ff.; star of, 133

Bethlehem, Pa., 108

Bible, King James, 22 q.

Blessing of homes, 173 f.

"Boar's Head," 143

Bohemia, Duke of, 80

Bonaventure, St., 87

Boniface, St., 36

Book of Wisdom, 51 q.

Boston, 48, 90, 92, 97, 98, 171

Boston Common, 122

Boston University School of Theology, 86

"Boxing," 159

Bradford, Governor, 48 q.

Braga, council of, 35

Breads, Christmas, 135 ff.

Brebeuf, John de, S.J., 82 f.

Breslau, Germany, 172

Britain, 55, 125, 126, 143, 144, 147, 159, 164, 171

British Isles, 125, 126

Brooks, Phillips, 84

Calendar, 18; Gregorian, 32; Julian, 33, 115

Calkin, John Baptist, 86

Calvinists, 79, 164

Canada, 38, 102; French, 92, 139, 140 f., 161

Candlemas day, 173 f.

Candles, 111 ff., 119, 168

Canterbury, 45

Canzonetta, 169

Canute, St., 140

"Carol of the children of Bethlehem," 64

Carols, Christmas, 37, 46, 55 ff., 79 ff.; companion carols, 70 f.; dance carols, 71 ff.; Epiphany carols, 74; lullaby carols, 68 ff.; macaronics, 67 f.; mystery carols, 65 f.; Nativity carols, 60 ff.; Noels, 67; prayer carols, 64 ff.; shepherd carols, 66 f.; star carols, 76; yodel carols, 76 ff.

Capitoline Hill, 109, 110

Catechism, 152 f.

Central America, 133, 140, 161, 170

Cham, 25

Chapel of the Manger, 34

Charles the Great, 35

Chaucer, *Romaunt of the Rose,* 56 q.

Cherry, 131 ff.

"Cherry tree carol," 132 f.

Chester, England, 68

Chesterton, G. K., 88

Child, 23, 70, 95, 96, 131; of Bethlehem, 47, 107; Divine, 32, 38, 53, 59, 65, 76, 98, 127, 160; Holy, 64, 68, 109, 133, 138, 161, 170, 171, 174; Jesus, 168; *see also* Christ Child

Children, patron saint of, *see* Nicholas, St.

Children's Sermon, 109

Christ, 17, 18, 21, 32, 51, 54, 60, 72, 94, 109, 111, 119, 126, 130, 137, 138, 154, 167, 173

"Christ-bundles," 158

Christ Child, 24, 40, 41, 44, 52, 75, 134, 152, 154, 157, 160, 161, 162, 166, 168, 170; *see also* Child

"Christ-rod," 158

"Christ was born in Bethlehem, and Mary was his niece," 86

Christianity, 19, 26, 36, 37, 126, 136, 142

Christians, 25, 31, 33, 34, 111, 123, 127, 130, 155

Christkindel, 161

"Christmas Bells," 85

Christmas Carol, 149

Christmas Man, 163, 164, 165

Christmas, names of, 28 ff.

Christmas outlawed, 44 ff.

Christmas Oratorio, 81

"Christmas ship," 158

Christmas Stories, 47

Chrysostom, St. John, 33 q.

Civil War, 85

Cole, Sir Henry, 171

Collectanea et Flores, 26 q.

Cologne, 26

Columban, St., 36

Constantine the Great, 19, 153, 155

Constantinople, 26, 35

Cornwall, 148

Cradle-rocking, 75 f.

Crèche, *see* Crib, Christmas

Crib, Christmas, 20, 23, 49, 53, 73, 77, 99, 105 ff., 122, 160, 161, 170, 173

Crusaders, 101, 147

Cummings, William H., 80

Cyprian, St., 33 q.

Cyril, St., 36

Czechs, 131

Dead Sea, 27

Decline and Fall of the Roman Empire, 109

Detroit, 84

Dickens, Charles, 109, 121 q., 129 q.; *Christmas Carol*, 149; *Christmas Stories*, 47

Dinner, Christmas, 142 ff.

Diocletian, Emperor, 153, 155

Dionysius Exiguus, 18

Divine Office, 43, 56, 86

Douay, France, 87

Drinking, 145 f.

Druids, 125, 126

Dwight, John Sullivan, 87

Eckhardt, John, 59

Eden, garden of, 118

Egley, William Maw, 171

Egypt, 18, 51, 131, 162

El Niño Jesús ha nacido ya, 90 f.

Elias, St., 137

England, 36, 37, 44, 53, 66, 71, 76, 79, 112, 115, 116, 120, 121, 124, 127, 129, 138, 140, 142, 144, 145, 148, 158, 163, 165

Eujalran, Father Jean, 102 ff. q.

Epiphany, 31, 35, 74, 76, 100, 101, 102, 130, 140, 161, 162, 173; octave of, 110, 173

Europe, 36, 43, 58, 96, 101, 119, 124, 126, 131, 135, 144, 152, 153, 160; Central, 49, 53, 107, 114, 131, 139, 152, 161; Eastern, 120, 136; Northern, 115, 127

Evangelists, 17

Eve, 118

Evergreens, 124

Evil One, 127

181

Falk, Johann, 82
Father Christmas, 164, 165
Feast of the Holy Innocents, 28
"Feast of the Star," 101
"Feast pig," 159
Fertility cults, 135, 137
Festgesang, 80
Fir, 124
Fires, Christmas, 114 ff.
"First Noel, The," 67
Firstborn, 21 f.
Flowers, Christmas, 123 ff.
Fonseca, Marcus Antonius, 87
Fourth of July, 170
France, 58, 66, 71, 76, 100, 112, 120, 138, 139, 140, 144, 161, 170; New, 91, 102; Southern, 28
Francis of Assisi, St., 40 q., 58, 105, 109
Franciscans, 58, 106
French, 38, 52, 140, 157; Canadians, 140
Friesland, 130
"From heaven above I come to you," 81

Gall, St., 36
Gaspar, 26, 173
"Gates of heaven's glory did spring open suddenly, The," 70
Genesis, 118
German-Americans, 108, 121
German Empire, 153
German immigration, 161
Germanic tribes, 116

Germans, 49; Catholics, 122; immigrants, 120, 122; Lutherans, 44, 81
Germany, 36, 49, 52, 58, 66, 75, 76, 81, 82, 89, 97, 107, 112, 117, 120, 127, 130, 138, 139, 154, 158, 159, 161, 168
Gesu Bambino, 87 f.
Gibbon, *Decline and Fall of the Roman Empire*, 109
Gifts, *see* Presents, Christmas
"Gloria," 86
God, 21, 38, 42, 107, 127, 131, 137, 154, 155, 173; Son of, 91
"God Eternal," 61
"God rest you merry, gentlemen," 30
"Good King Wenceslaus," 80
Greccio, Italy, 106, 107
Greece, 154
Greek Church, 153
Greeks, 55
Greeting cards, 171 ff.
Gregory I, Pope St., 124; *Libri Miraculorum*, 39
Gregory XIII, Pope, 32 f., 115
Grey, Hon. Sir Henry, 144
Gruber, Franz, 89, 90

Habakkuk, 109 q.
Hadrian, Emperor, 19
Handel, *Messiah*, 58, 81; *Siroe*, 80
Hanukkah, 111
"Hark, the herald angels sing," 80
Harrison, *Sketches of Upper Canada*, 38

Harrison, President, 121 q.
Helen of Mecklenburg, Princess, 120
Herbergsuchen, 98 f.
Herod, King, 18, 26, 93, 101
Herrick, Robert, 115 q., 130 q., 148, 174 q.; "Twelfe Night," 141 q.
Hilary, St., 57
Holland, 76, 154, 159, 163 f.
Holly, 124, 126 ff.
Holy City, 110
Holy Eucharist, 43, 118
Holy Family, 98, 162
Holy Land, 101, 148, 154
Holy Night, 113, 114, 115, 138, 139, 161, 162, 170, 171
Holy Trinity church, Boston, 97, 98
Holy Trinity church, Philadelphia, 85
Holy Week, 111
Hone, William, Ancient Mysteries, 80 q.
Hopkins, John Henry, Jr., 85
Horsley, J. C., 171
Hudson, 164
Hungary, 36, 92
"Hunter's Carol," 70 f.
Huron Indians, 82, 91, 102
Huron, Lake, 102
Hymns, Christmas, 55 ff., 79 ff.
Hyrcania, 27

In dulci Jubilo, 174
"In the circle of this year," 57
India, 25
Indians, 38, 102

Infant, the Divine, 104, 106; see also Child; Christ Child
Ipswich, 45
Iran, 25
Iraq, 25
Ireland, 36, 53, 66, 112, 113, 138
Irish, 41, 47 f., 113; immigrants, 131
Iroquois, 82, 83
Irving, Washington, Sketch Book, 47
Isaiah, 25 q., 109 q.
Israel, 109
"It came upon the midnight clear," 84
Italy, 28, 58, 66, 106, 107, 140, 154, 161; shepherds in, 169
Ivy, 127, 128 ff.

Japhet, 25
Jericho, 27
Jerome, St., 19 q., 20 q.
Jerusalem, 20
Jesuit Fathers, 97
Jesuit Relations, 102
Jesus, 102, 103, 104, 106, 107, 131, 149, 160, 161
"Jesus is born," 82
"Jesus, Light of all the nations," 57
Jews, 21, 27, 111
John, 106
John the Evangelist, St., 146
Jordan, 38
Joseph, St., 18, 19, 23, 24, 70, 98, 100, 114, 132, 133
Joseph, uncle of King Herod, 27

"Joy to the world! The Lord is come," 80
Julius Caesar, 33
Justin the Martyr, St., 19 q.
Justinian, Emperor, 20, 35

Kent, 45
Kentucky mountains, 86
"Kings' Cake," 140
"Kings, The," 74
Kirkpatrick, William James, 82
Kolya, 162
Kostobar, 27
Kris Kringle, 161

Latin countries, 90, 145
Laurel, 123, 124, 130 f.
Lebanon valley, 121
Legends, Christmas, 37 ff., 50, 54, 166
Leipzig, 90
Leo I, Pope St., 34
Leo III, Pope, 35
"Let every age and nation know," 57
Letter-writing, 168
Libri Miraculorum, 39
Lights, Christmas, 111 ff.
Lithuania, 39
Lithuanians, 138, 140
Log, Christmas, *see* Yule log
London, 45, 87, 144
Longfellow, Henry Wadsworth, 85 q., 86
Loretto, 83
Lorraine, 154
Luke, St., 17, 53 q., 111 q.

Luther, Martin, 81, 82, 122
Lutherans, 81, 122

Macaronics, *see* Carols
Mackinac, Michigan, 91
Madonna, 169; *see also* Mary; Mother of God; Virgin
Magi, 24 ff., 74, 76, 93, 130, 140, 162, 173; Well of the, 39
Mainz, 37
Manhattan Island, 164
Mariamne, 27
Marlatt, Earl, 86
Marten, Frederick, 87
Mary, Mother of God, 18, 19, 21, 23, 40, 41, 68, 70, 95, 98, 100, 104, 114, 127, 131, 132; *see also* Virgin
Maryland, My Maryland, 82
Mason, Lowell, 81
Mass, Christmas, 29, 34, 43, 49, 51 ff., 86, 103, 113, 114, 138
Matthew, St., 17, 24, 25 q., 27 f. q., 157 q.
Medfield, Massachusetts, 81
Media, 24
Melchior, 26, 173
Mendelssohn, 84; *Festgesang,* 80
Messiah, 58, 81
Methodist revival, 84
Methodius, St., 36
Mexico, 99, 124, 133, 144, 170
Middle Ages, 153
Middleton, J. E., 83
Milan, 26, 101
Mince pie, 147 ff.; "battle of," 149 ff.

"Miracle play," *see* Plays, Christmas

Mistletoe, 124, 125 f.

Mithras cult, 33

Mohammedans, 20

Mohr, Joseph, 89, 90

Moore, " 'Twas the Night Before Christmas," 165

Moravians, 108

Moses, 127

Mother of God, 169; *see also* Madonna; Mary; Virgin

Murray, James R., 81

Myra, 152, 155; Bishop of, *see* Nicholas, St.

"Mystery," 94

Mystery plays, *see* Play, Christmas

Nativity, 18 ff., 31, 37, 49, 56, 57, 60, 92, 102, 105, 111, 112, 139, 142, 174; feast of, 31 ff.; plays and pageants, 94 ff.

Nativity, 23

Nativity, church of, 20, 53

Nazareth, 20

Neale, John M., 80

New Amsterdam, 164

New England, 48, 49, 121, 147, 150, 165

New Testament, 23

New World, 143, 145, 164

New York, 120, 121, 161, 164, 165

Nicholas, St., 139, 152, 160, 163, 164, 165, 166; legend of, 154 ff.

Noels, *see* Carols

North Pole, 165

Novena, 170

"Now it is Christmas again," 72 f.

"O Christmas tree," 82

"O come, all ye children," 82

"O come, all ye Faithful," 53

"O gladsome Light," 57

"O Holy Night," 87

"O little town of Bethlehem," 84 f.

"O royal day of holy joy," 57

"O thou joyful Christmastime," 82

Oakely, Dr. Frederick, 87

Oberndorf, 88

Ocumare de la Costa, Venezuela, 90

"Of the Father's love begotten," 57

"Office of the Star," 100

Ohio, 121

Old Testament, 109

Orient, 25, 38

Origen, 19

Orleans, Duke of, 120

Oxford, 45

Pageants, Christmas, 97 ff., 163

Palatinate, 120

Palestine, 19, 20, 24

Paradise, 41, 118; play, 117; tree, 118

Parara, 154

Paris, 120; Conservatory of Music, 87

Parliament, 45 q.

Pastries, Christmas, 119, 135 ff.

Patrick, St., 36
Pelznickel, 163
Pennsylvania, 81, 108, 120 f.;
   Dutch, 163
Persia, 24, 25
Persians, 20
Peter, St., 137
Peter's, St., 35
Philadelphia, 81
Pifferari, 86, 169
Pilgrim fathers, 48
Piñata, 100
Pius IX, Pope, 65 q.
Plants, Christmas, 123 ff.
Plays, Christmas, 37, 75, 94 ff.
Plum pudding, 148 f.
Poinsett, Dr. Joel Roberts, 133
Poinsettia, 125, 133 f.
Poitiers, 57
Poland, 49, 92, 137
Poles, 112, 138, 171
Poor Robin's Almanack, 47 q.
Portogallo, 87
Portugal, 28, 140; king of, 87
Posada, 99 f., 169, 170
Prang, Louis, 171 f.
Presents, Christmas, 157 ff.
Prudentius, 57
Psalms, 25 q.
Psalmus in Nativite, 58
Puritans, 44, 79, 147, 149, 150
"Putzing," 108

Quando noctis medium, 52
Quebec, 83, 102
Qui creavit caelum, 68

Radburn, New Jersey, 83
Rainers, 88

Redner, Louis H., 85
Reformation, 43, 71, 76, 79, 97,
   101, 108, 126, 149, 163
Rhine, 119, 122; provinces, 120
Ring-dances, 55, 56, 71, 72
"Rise up, shepherd, an' foller,"
   87
Roman Empire, 35, 123, 155
Romans, 19, 33, 55, 169
Romaunt of the Rose, 56 q.
Rome, 18, 34, 105, 109, 128, 130,
   157, 161, 169; Church in, 32
Roquemaure, M. Cappeau de, 87
Rosemary, 124, 131
Rouen, Cathedral of, 94
Rumanians, 138
Russia, 139, 154, 162
Russians, 112, 138

Sabinum, 169
St. Eustorgius, church of, 101
St. Ignace, Michigan, 102
St. John's Day, 146
St. Louis, 92
St. Mary Major, church of, 35
St. Mary of the Nativity, 20
St. Mary's Abbey, 68
St. Patrick's Cathedral, New York,
   87 f.
St. Sebastian's Catacombs, 105
Salzburg, 88
San Nicola, church of, 153
Santa Claus, 160, 161, 165, 172
Saturnalia, 123
Saviour, 118, 149, 169; *see also*
   Jesus; Christ
Scandinavia, 72
Scandinavians, 36, 140

Schmid, Christoph von, 82

Schulz, Johann A. P., 82

Scotland, 44, 53, 138

Sears, Edmund H., 84

Sem, 25

Seville, Cathedral of, 71

Sewa, 26

Shakespeare, 40 f. q.

Shepherds, 23, 66 f., 70, 73, 77, 169

Sicily, 154

"Silent Night," *see Stille Nacht*

Sinter Klaas, 164

Siroe, 80

Sketch Book, 47

Sketches of Upper Canada, 38

Slavic countries, 69, 76, 92, 112, 138, 170 f.

Slavs, 36, 66, 120

Slovaks, 131

"Snow lay on the ground, The," 86

South America, 90, 99, 107, 112, 140, 161, 169, 170

South Carolina, 133

Spain, 28, 52, 58, 66, 71, 90, 140, 144, 161

"Spotless rose is growing, A," 57

Spruce, 124

Stephen, St., 159

Sternsingen, 76, 102

Stille Nacht, Heilige Nacht, 88 ff.

Strasbourg, 120

Strenae, 157

Superstitions, 37 ff., 127

Suso, Blessed Henry, 59; *In dulci Jubilo*, 174 q.

Switzerland, 36, 115, 139, 154

Tauler, John, 59

Taylor, John, 150 q.

Tate, Nahum, 80

Temple, Rededication of the, 111

Tenebrae services, 111

Tertullian, 34, 123 f. q.

Thanksgiving, 147, 172

Theodosius, Emperor, 35

Thomas the Apostle, St., 26

Thomas of Celano, 58 q., 106 f. q.

Thomas, Edith Lovell, 83

Thor, 116

"Thou camest from the Heavens," 65

"Three Kings, The," 101 f.

Toledo, 71

Toronto, 83

Trapp singers, 88

Tree, Christmas, 49, 112, 117 ff.

Trinity, 112

Trinity church, Boston, 84

Tours, 39; council of, 35

Turkeys, 145

" 'Twas the Night Before Christmas," 165

"Twelfe Night," 141 q.

Tyrol, 39, 70, 75, 76, 77, 88, 131

Ukrainians, 61, 112, 136, 171

United States, 151, 161

Velitta, Messer Giovanni, 106

Venantius Fortunatus, 57

Venezuela, 140

Venus, 19

Victoria, Queen, 120

Vienna, 108

187

Villeneuve, Father Etienne de, 83

Vimont, Father Bartholomew, S.J., 91 q.

Virgin, 104; Blessed, 83, 137; *see also* Madonna; Mary; Mother of God

Vulgate, 22 q.

Wade, John Francis, 87

Wales, 28

"Waltham," 86

Waltham Abbey, England, 80

"Wassail," 145

Watts, Isaac, 81

"We three kings of Orient are," 85

Wenceslaus, St., 80

Wesley, Charles, 80

Weston, Massachusetts, 84

"While shepherds watched their flocks by night," 79 f.

Whistlecraft, 143 q.

White House, 121

Willis, Richard Storrs, 80, 84

Windsor Castle, 120

Wisconsin, 121

World War II, 108

"World's desire, The," 88

Yew, 124

Yodeling, 76 ff.; *see also* Carols

Yon, Pietro, 87

York, Cathedral of, 126; Minster of, 71

Yule, 29; log, 115, 116